WOMEN'S UNITED SOCCER ASSOCIATION

GIRL'S
GUIDE TO
SOCCER
LIFE

WOMEN'S UNITED SOCCER ASSOCIATION

GIRL'S GUIDE TO SOCCER LIFE

By the Stars of the WUSA

COOL SPRINGS PRESS

Nashville, Tennessee
A Division of Thomas Nelson, Inc.
www.ThomasNelson.com

All photography provided by Getty Images.

Published by Cool Springs Press, a Division of Thomas Nelson, Inc., P.O. Box 141000, Nashville, Tennessee, 37214

Library of Congress Cataloging-in-Publication Data is available. ISBN 1-591860-40-7

First printing 2003
Printed in the United States of America
10 9 8 7 6 5 4 3 2 1

Editor: Ramona D. Wilkes
Copyeditor: Jason Zasky
Proofing: Sally Graham
Production/Design: Brian David Smith

Visit the Thomas Nelson website at www.ThomasNelson.com

Table of Contents

Foreword

Lynn Morgan

Featuring the best players from 14 different countries, the Women's United Soccer Association (WUSA) is the premier women's soccer league in the world. Nearly 50 WUSA athletes will compete in the 2003 FIFA Women's World Cup.

World Cup and Olympic champions such as Washington's Mia Hamm, New York's Tiffeny Milbrett, San Jose's Brandi Chastain, Boston's Kristine Lilly, San Diego's Julie Foudy, and Atlanta's Briana Scurry are fan favorites, and rising stars such as San Diego's Aly Wagner and Washington's Abby Wambach are making an impact on the international soccer scene. In addition, Philadelphia's Marinette Pichon (France), San Jose's Katia (Brazil), Carolina's Hege Riise (Norway), and Birgit Prinz (Germany) are just a few of the more than two dozen international stars competing in the WUSA.

Following the success of the 1999 Women's World Cup, the WUSA began play in 2001, and the league's players have formed a relationship like no other in sports. We set out with two important goals in mind. First, to bring women's professional soccer to the forefront of American sports, and second, to become positive role models for children everywhere. With the participation of every professional member of the U.S. Women's National Team and the very best international stars from around the globe, the WUSA is achieving those goals.

While WUSA players have the opportunity to play the game they love and make a living doing so, they also realize they can bring positive change to the youth of America. Being a role model and positively influencing children is something that the WUSA and its players see as a remarkable opportunity. Community service and charity is something that the league—including every player, team, and general manager—treats as a top priority.

With that same spirit more than 40 WUSA players have contributed to this book. From their own words you will learn from these out-standing women about the game they love and what it takes to be successful both on and off the field. Whether you are a player, parent, or coach, there is something for you in the ***WUSA Girl's Guide to Soccer Life***. In addition, the accompanying DVD contains an exciting mix of the WUSA's greatest highlights, and comments from some of the league's best-known players.

In an era where the number of young women competing in sports continues to grow, the WUSA and WUSA Players Association is proud to present this unique combination of media that is sure to give you new insight into the game we all love.

Enjoy.

Lynn Morgan
President & Chief Executive Officer
Women's United Soccer Association
www.WUSA.com

Introduction

Tony DiCicco

Prior to the 1996 Olympic Gold Medal game and the 1999 World Cup Final, I wrote the following message on the flipchart in our locker room: *Play hard, play fair, play to win, and HAVE FUN.* This, in one short sentence, encapsulates my philosophy of coaching. It wasn't an accident that I emphasized, "Have Fun." Whether you are a seven-year-old getting your first taste of learning how to kick a ball or a professional playing in the WUSA, the soccer and the overall experience has to be enjoyable. Unfortunately, many coaches take the fun and therefore the learning out of the game. I saw my own coaching evolve during my time as head coach of the U.S. Women's National Team. Early on, I attempted to motivate through my own intensity. But I developed as a coach and learned from a special group of talented and motivated young women. The rest, as they say, is history. Together we won the first-ever Olympic Gold medal in women's soccer and were part of the greatest women's sporting event in history, the 1999 FIFA Women's World Cup.

Today, the world looks at female athletes and women in team sports differently, and the U.S. Women's National Team has played a big role in that cultural shift. Many of the women who went on to win the 1996 Olympic gold medal and the 1999 World Cup trophy provide their perspective on soccer and life in this important book. Their stories are unique and inspiring.

In addition, some of the great international players and the next generation of stars contribute their thoughts and ideas on many aspects of the game and life within the game. Topics include: how to get started; ways to improve; how to organize training on your own; and creating your own personal dream. Moreover, items such as dealing with coaches and parents, and overcoming setbacks (such as injuries or being cut from a team) are also addressed.

In total, more than 40 stars of the WUSA provide their insight into soccer on and off the field. How do you manage your time? What should you eat? Even what to do with your hair.

The **WUSA Girl's Guide to Soccer Life** and its accompanying DVD are essential reading and viewing material. Never before has there been such a valuable compilation of information from the best soccer players in the world. Just as my coaching evolved by working with and learning from these players, you too will be rewarded with insights that will inspire, motivate and assist you to be a better player, coach, or soccer parent.

Tony DiCicco
Commissioner, Women's United Soccer Association
Head Coach, U.S. Women's National Team (1994 –99)
'96 Olympic Gold Medallists; '99 World Champions

United Church of Christ
at Valley Forge
45 Walker Road
Wayne, PA   19087

MEMORIES
OF GETTING
STARTED

*It was love
at first kick!*

—Brandi Chastain

TONY DiCICCO

Many WUSA players started soccer when they were very young. When you start playing soccer, first you learn to be with a team. You learn how to be competitive and what it feels like to win. You also learn what it's like to lose and how to deal with those emotions. You learn to fall down and get back up. You learn how it feels to keep running when you're tired and winded. When you're getting started in soccer it's probably going to be a little bit scary... but fun too!

Mia Hamm

I started playing organized soccer when I was five. I had an older brother and two older sisters who played. My dad coached us and would referee games. We pretty much spent every Saturday out on the field.

Brandi Chastain

I was six, and my parents realized early on that I enjoyed being outside and being very active. They first put me into dance class with some neighborhood girls. Though dance was all right I don't think it was enough for me. It just so happened that an all-girls soccer league was starting up. I walked down one block from my house and signed up at the local school. That's basically how it began. Nobody knew anything

MY MOTTO

"Respect yourself"

-Mia Hamm

about the game in my family, but we all jumped in two feet into the fire.

Julie Foudy

I was six when I first started playing soccer with some boys in my elementary school. There was no girls team until I was seven, so I had to wait a year before I could play on a real team.

Cindy Parlow

My dad was coaching my two older brothers, so I joined that team.

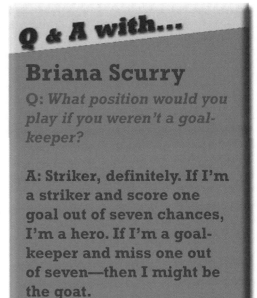

Q & A with...

Briana Scurry

Q: *What position would you play if you weren't a goalkeeper?*

A: Striker, definitely. If I'm a striker and score one goal out of seven chances, I'm a hero. If I'm a goalkeeper and miss one out of seven—then I might be the goat.

Carla Overbeck

I liked playing soccer because my two older brothers and older sister all played.

Tiffany Roberts

My family is very sports oriented. My dad was an athlete, and he threw me and my three older brothers into sports. He got me started in soccer, track, and gymnastics.

Joy Fawcett

I started playing when I was five years old. I have eight brothers and sisters and everyone played, so I just kind of followed along with the family.

Abby Wambach

I'm the youngest of seven, and all my brothers and sisters played sports. I started playing organized soccer when I was five.

Our Favorites

Things to Wear

Danielle Slaton
Jeans and a white t-shirt

Shannon MacMillan
Red nail polish

Charmaine Hooper
Stud earrings

 ## Briana Scurry

I got started in soccer when I was twelve. There was a bunch of flyers sent around my classroom about different sports and soccer was one of them. So I picked up a flyer, brought it home, and my Mom and Dad said I could play. I'm from Anoka, which is a really small community in Minnesota. We didn't have a girls team, so I was the only girl on the boys team, and they put me in as the goalkeeper. The following year I had to travel 45 minutes each way to play on a girls team.

 ## Charmaine Hooper

My brother played soccer. He's about a year older than I am. Everything he did I did. My family actually moved from Guyana (South America) to Zambia (Africa) when I was seven. Zambia is where I first played the game, but just for fun with other kids. We moved from Zambia to Canada when I was ten. I was twelve, when riding my bike I saw a group of girls playing an organized game of soccer. I had never seen that before. That's when I got involved.

 ## Katia

I started playing soccer in Brazil when I was 18 years old. We played on the street, and I was the only girl playing against all boys.

Sissi

The only way to play five to seven years ago in Brazil was with the boys because the girls were kind of shy about it. People said soccer was just for men, not for women.

Marinette Pichon

I started playing soccer with the boys because growing up in France there were no girls teams. I remember the first time I played, the boys mocked me and said, "You're a girl. You can't play with us." After they threw me the ball and saw that I could play the game they said, "All right, we want you on our team." That was very funny.

Mary McVeigh

I was four years old when I first started. My older brother is a year and a half older than I am. We played in a co-ed league that my dad coached. It was a pretty standard beginning.

When I was six we moved to Germany for two years, and I played on a boys team over there. That's when I became passionate about soccer. There weren't many girls teams back then. It was a lot tougher playing against the boys. And we didn't play on grass in Germany, we played on gravel. So when I came back to the States two years later I was sliding all over the place and pushing people around. When I came back, the league that I played in actually made a rule against slide tackling because of me.

> **Did You Know?**
>
> When **Shannon MacMillan** has free time, she likes to work on her scrapbook. She has "tons" of pictures, and sometimes she and teammate Joy Fawcett work on it together.

Did You Know?

Julie Foudy was accepted into the prestigious Stanford Medical School but decided not to pursue medicine.

Angela Hucles

I was six years old when my mom signed me up for the neighborhood swim team. I didn't like it much because it was a freezing cold pool and I had to get up in the morning to go to swim practice. I'm not a morning person. The following season she signed me up for soccer, and I've been playing ever since.

Leslie Gaston

I started playing in Mississippi. My parents played sports growing up, and they basically sat me up on the counter and asked which sport I wanted to play. I started doing tap and jazz, but when this little boy stepped on my fingers I didn't want to do that anymore! So I decided to play soccer, and I played on a boys team in Mississippi.

Tiffeny Milbrett

My mom played soccer, so I was very fortunate to have that influence. I grew up on the sidelines of her practices and games and bugged her until I was old enough to be on a team.

These days professional sports have *become big business.*

A lot of pro athletes play only to make a lot of money. But the players in the WUSA started playing because we genuinely loved to play the game.

Brandi Chastain

It was love at first kick! It just felt natural for me right away. I enjoyed spending time by myself with the ball, and I enjoyed the camaraderie with my teammates and the challenge of the game.

Mia Hamm

I loved the freeness of it all. You've got a pretty big field, and you're outdoors, experiencing all the sights and sounds of everything that's going on. Plus you're out there with your friends!

Julie Foudy

I liked practice to begin with. I liked that it required a lot physically and that there was a lot of running around. I also loved that it was a team sport. I played on the same team for ten years growing up, and a lot of those guys are still my best friends.

Briana Scurry

In soccer there are eleven players on a team working together. I always liked the idea of that. It wasn't my favorite sport when I was younger, but I think the friendships and working together were very appealing to me.

Most Embarrassing Moment

"When I was 16, I was running late to a game and was going to have to put my uniform on when I got to the game site. When the referee was checking me in, I took off my sweats and realized I had forgotten to put on my shorts! It was just me and my Daffy Duck™ underwear!"

– Lorrie Fair

Tiffany Roberts

All my best friends were on the team, and I really enjoyed spending time with them. We would get together at practice and gossip. Then we would have pizza parties and slumber parties. When you travel together with a team, you really develop strong relationships with your teammates.

Joy Fawcett

Besides the friendships and being able to play as a team, I loved working on all the little technical stuff and the individual moves. I remember doing that all day in my backyard.

Jennifer Grubb

I liked that it was a skill game. You can learn to play even if you're not the fastest or the strongest kid. I think more people can play because of that.

Tisha Venturini-Hoch

I think I liked being able to be physical and run around and be creative. There weren't set plays, just whatever happened, happened.

Angela Hucles

For me it was physically challenging. It was a contact sport, but it was safe. I think growing up I liked that the players just got to play without the coaches stopping every five seconds to call the next play.

Shannon MacMillan

I played for the orange slices and the juice boxes at halftime and after the game!

Kylie Bivens

In the beginning, I played defense, and I just picked flowers all the time. I liked the snacks you got at halftime and at the end of the game.

Mary McVeigh

What's not to like? I mean you get to go out and run around and compete. You get to make friends. Certainly as a young kid that's really all you want out of life at that point.

As WUSA players, we have seen the sport of women's soccer become huge! In 1981 there were only 17 NCAA Division 1 schools playing women's soccer. Today there are 286!

Many of us got started in soccer at an early age, playing any way we could. Besides the game and the friendships, there were many reasons we liked being around the soccer field.

Shannon MacMillan

When you first start out it's called bumblebee ball, where the whole "hive" chases the ball!

Kylie Bivens

I remember bunch ball. Everybody would be crowding around the ball, and we would all be trying to kick it.

Lorrie Fair

My dad was always my coach. I remember there was a muddy, muddy game and the ball plopped right in the middle of the mud puddle. All ten field players were standing around the mud puddle. All of a sudden my dad yells from the sidelines, "Lorrie, what are you doing? Go ahead and get it!" and I ran straight through the mud puddle and kicked the ball. My pant leg ripped, and I was covered in mud. My dad had to hose me off before my mom would let me in the house.

Aly Wagner

I was playing against two of my current best friends. We were about seven. The game went back and forth, back and forth. They scored. We scored. They scored. We scored. The game ended in a 7-7 tie. I scored all my team's goals. My friends scored their team's goals too, and we all cried at the end.

Leslie Gaston

There was only one other girl on my team, and sometimes the soccer part wasn't as interesting as being friends. We ran around the field holding hands and just kind of forgot about the ball.

Danielle Slaton

When I was five or six I started by playing in goal. I was the only girl on the team, and the boys really didn't want me to play with them. I remember that I used to just pick flowers and not pay attention to the game at all. There is this one picture that my father has of me. He was taking pictures of me during the game, and he yelled, "Danielle, look over here!" In the picture you see me posing as the ball is flying by into the back of the net!

Our Favorites

Foods

Brandi Chastain
Thai food

Callie Withers
Scrambled eggs

Leslie Gaston
Ice cream

Homare Sawa
Japanese rice

Charmaine Hooper
Mexican food

Nel Fettig

I played with boys growing up. So high-fiving the boys and having them high-five me back was neat. Nowadays I'll see these guys I played with when I was six, and they'll say, "That's so great that you play soccer."

Lorrie Fair

Katia

Angela Hucles

I remember the first neighborhood team I played for was the Stingers, and I was the only girl on the team. It felt pretty special being the only girl, especially since I was the primary goal scorer.

Jennifer Grubb

I played on a mixed boys and girls team. There were a few girls and the rest boys. I remember my coach making a statement that girls couldn't play soccer. So now I kind of wish that I could find him and let him know that I can!

Marinette Pichon

When I was 12, we played in a tournament, and I remember the other team saying, "Oh, she's a girl. She can't score." Well, I scored the only goal of the game, and we won one to zero!

Shannon MacMillan

I remember the road trips when I first got on a traveling team—getting in the big vans with the families and heading out—and the slumber parties we had the night before the games.

Breanna Boyd

I have lots of memories of traveling with teams when I was younger. I really enjoyed that. I remember one time the team got stuck in an elevator!

Christie Welsh

I remember sleepovers and parties and just talking with my teammates. As I got older my teammates were coming from all over Long Island, New York. Knowing people from all different places was great. I even made friends with girls from different countries. So those memories were definitely the coolest things to have from my childhood.

Brandi Chastain

When I was six, the night I received my first uniform I slept in it. I didn't want to take it off after trying it on. I remember it was red, white, and blue. We were named the Quakes after the NASL's San Jose Earthquakes.

Carla Overbeck

I would always sleep in my uniform the night before a tournament. I'd wake up, eat my cereal, watch some cartoons, and be ready and waiting to go.

Kristine Lilly

My fondest memories were waiting each year to see what colors my team was going to wear. We didn't have high-tech uniforms, they were just T-shirts. Every game day, I'd wake up, and the first thing I'd do was put my uniform on.

Briana Scurry

Tisha Venturini-Hoch

My first year I played on the Koalas. Our colors were orange and blue. I remember putting that uniform on. That was the coolest part, along with having shin guards and the shoes. I didn't really care so much about the game. I just wanted to wear that uniform.

Carrie Moore

I was seven and playing on a team called the Cardinals. We had red uniforms, and I had red bow ribbons in my hair that my mom had dressed me up in. I got yelled at by the referee and had to take them out.

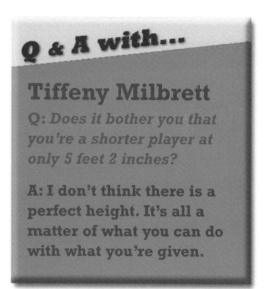

Q & A with...

Tiffeny Milbrett

Q: *Does it bother you that you're a shorter player at only 5 feet 2 inches?*

A: I don't think there is a perfect height. It's all a matter of what you can do with what you're given.

Julie Foudy

One of my best memories is of juggling a ball 150 times! I got a 12-scoop ice cream sundae for doing that.

When we were growing up, there was no women's World Cup and no women's soccer in the Olympic Games. *The WUSA was not even a blip on the sports radar screen. For most of us, our family's influence was very important when we were getting started.*

Mia Hamm

I had an older brother and two older sisters who played. I remember it was all about trying to be like them.

Aly Wagner

My older sister was always someone I looked up to when I was younger just because she was always the older soccer player and doing more exciting things than I was. I was always trying to do things like her, and I'd go out to her team's practices and play with them. There's a big difference in ability between nine and eleven years of age. So I think it really forced me to be a better player.

Tiffeny Milbrett

My mom was my biggest influence. She played soccer, so every time I got to go to her practices or her games I just remember being so excited. I really think having a mom as an athlete was key because all we did was play. Without that influence I would be a different person.

Lorrie Fair

My dad got me started in sports. He was the kind of father who didn't really know much about sports, but he would go out and buy a book about a sport and then teach me the basics. When he felt like he ran out of expertise, he would find somebody who had more knowledge. He taught me everything about basketball, and I also tried volleyball and softball. He used to have me try everything.

Marinette Pichon

My mom provided me with a lot of support. I was just one girl playing with all boys, and she would bring me to the parties and the games, not to mention wash my uniform and my cleats.

Angela Hucles

My parents introduced things to me and then let me just go with it. I think without their support I probably wouldn't have been able to stick with soccer. It would have been a

Carla Overbeck

lot more challenging to be involved in things like the Olympic development program and travel soccer. But it was really a family-oriented activity for us growing up.

Danielle Slaton

I think my parents influenced me by giving me the freedom to decide what I wanted to do. My father was a track coach, and my mom danced. To have to tell them that I didn't want to do track anymore, that I didn't want to do ballet anymore—I think was kind of hard for them, but they definitely gave me the freedom to choose what I wanted to do. So in that sense I really appreciate them for letting me decide what I liked to do best.

Cindy Parlow

My parents taught us we could do anything that we wanted to do. Male, female, short or tall—it didn't matter. You were capable of doing anything.

Kristin Luckenbill

My parents were so in support of athletics. When I was really little—I couldn't even walk yet—my dad would knock a golf ball around the floor with a putter, and I would chase after it like some kind of little pet. It's funny that I'm still sort of doing that today. Still chasing a ball!

Shannon MacMillan

My brother was a big influence on me. He actually didn't stick with soccer too long, but all of his buddies would come to the door, and the first thing they'd say is, "Hey, can your sister come out and play street hockey?" He'd say, "Wait a minute. These are MY friends." But once we got out there, he definitely made sure that I was on his team because he didn't want to be going against me. Whatever I tried, he really inspired me to go after it and to believe in myself. He was an inspiration. I remember when I left for college, he said, "This is your chance. Don't look back."

CHOOSING SOCCER

*In my case, the deciding
factor on playing soccer was
different than most.*

—Briana Scurry

TONY DiCICCO

I have four sons. One plays soccer 365 days a year and loves it. I have another son who plays soccer in the fall. It's one of his top sports, but he also plays basketball in the winter, he runs track, and he's in a band. If a child plays too much of any one sport, usually he or she will burn out. Most kids don't want to let anyone down, especially the adults in their lives. And when the coaches say, "Okay we're finishing our fall season, and we're going to play soccer indoors next week," kids don't want to say to them, "Hey coach I need a break."

Julie Foudy

In high school, I played volleyball, soccer, and ran track. Track was really just to stay fit for soccer and to socialize. It wasn't until college that I really focused on soccer.

Actually, I think soccer kind of chose me. That's the difference nowadays. A lot of us older players didn't have the role models and the big dreams of playing in Olympic soccer because there was no such thing. There wasn't even a World Cup until 1991. When I got onto the national team, I really didn't even know what the national team was.

We didn't know what to dream. True, I wanted to play in the Olympics, but I thought it would be in another sport. I think I always loved sports. I always loved being active. I always had an affinity for soccer, and I excelled at it. But it wasn't until college that I realized my potential.

Mia Hamm

I played basketball, baseball, and softball. Those were the main organized sports that I played. I also played all the sports that you usually play in your neighborhood, like football and stickball.

I probably chose soccer as my main sport when I made the national team at age 15. I wanted to stay involved with it as long as I could. It seemed that the soccer results mattered a lot more to me than the other sports, and I wasn't the best shooter in basketball. I was quick and fast and could steal the ball and make layups, but I couldn't really shoot the ball.

Brandi Chastain

I participated in track and field, softball, basketball, and dance. If tree climbing had been a sport then I would have participated in that too! I did all of those until I was a senior in high school, but I think I chose soccer because it felt the most natural to me. It became a part of what I did on a normal day.

Briana Scurry

I played basketball, softball, and I ran track. I played all four sports, including soccer, up until my junior year in high school.

In my case, the deciding factor on playing soccer was different than most. I got a lot of scholarships in high school for track, basketball, soccer, and a couple for softball. But I think when it really came down to it, I had to have a full scholarship because my parents couldn't afford spending a lot of money to help me. I was an All-state basketball player, but an All-American goalkeeper in soccer, so I had a lot more opportunities to play soccer. It just made more sense to go with that.

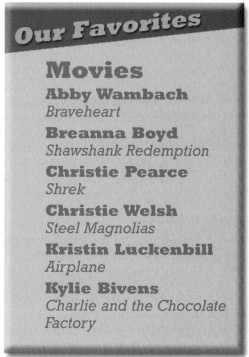

Our Favorites

Movies

Abby Wambach
Braveheart

Breanna Boyd
Shawshank Redemption

Christie Pearce
Shrek

Christie Welsh
Steel Magnolias

Kristin Luckenbill
Airplane

Kylie Bivens
Charlie and the Chocolate Factory

Shannon MacMillan

In basketball I was too short, and the net was too small for me. I played softball because I had speed. But if you can't hit the ball you are never on base. So I gave that up quickly. I tried track because the track coach at my high school begged me to come out and run. When I did I realized the shorts were way too short for mc! After about the third day, he looked at me and said, "You run like a soccer player." Then it just clicked, and I said, "I AM a soccer player!"

No matter what was going on at home or at school, even if I was having the worst day, as soon as I stepped across the line it was like I became free. All my troubles left me. Soccer was a sport that was not easy for me, but I enjoyed it the most, and it was the most natural for me.

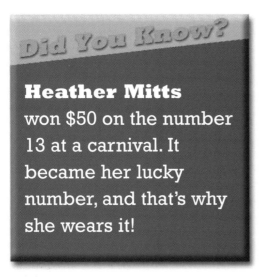

Did You Know?

Heather Mitts won $50 on the number 13 at a carnival. It became her lucky number, and that's why she wears it!

Nel Fettig

I played the gamut of sports: basketball, volleyball, gymnastics, and swimming. But the two sports that I was a serious competitor in were soccer and tennis. I stopped playing club soccer at the age of eleven. For two years I only played in the Olympic development program and focused mostly on tennis. Tennis is such a pressure sport and also very intense. It takes a lot of time.

Soccer is such a fun environment to be in. There's something in it for me that really drives me to play all the time, whether it's just with a friend in the backyard or practicing with as many teams as I can. There's something beautiful about the game that gets me out there on the field.

Kristin Luckenbill

I played t-ball and soccer, went snow skiing, and basically tried every sport that you can think of when I was growing up. Eventually things gradually narrowed down.

I was fortunate enough to have perfect timing. The WUSA started the year after my senior year in college. So I just happened to be in the right place at the right time. Prior to that there wasn't an outlet to play professionally. So it wasn't even a thought in my mind. I was just going to go get a job somewhere else doing something completely different. Then as soon as I heard about this league, I was still like, "No, no it won't happen." Then I got drafted. All of a sudden I was in training camp and saying, "Hey, all right. This is where I am, and this is what I'm doing, and I love it."

Tiffany Roberts

I stuck with soccer and track all the way through high school. I didn't love track, but my dad really liked it, and as I got older I realized it was good for my soccer. I also competed in gymnastics until I was about ten or eleven.

I probably started getting serious about soccer when people started telling me that I had something special and that I could go really far in soccer. I was in junior high, probably 13 years old, and I made the Northern California state team. I was a younger player trying out against older girls. When I made that team, I thought that was a really big deal. I thought, "Well, if I can make the state team, maybe I'm good enough to make the regional team," and so on....

Carrie Moore

When I was little I was on the swim team and played baseball. When I got to middle school I played basketball, volleyball, and ran track. Whatever was in season—I was going out for the team.

Soccer was just what I was best at. In high school I played volleyball for my school and did the junior Olympic volleyball program. I played basket-

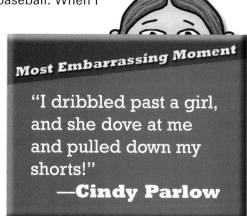

Most Embarrassing Moment

"I dribbled past a girl, and she dove at me and pulled down my shorts!"
—Cindy Parlow

ball, AAU, and did all the soccer stuff like the Olympic development program. I think that's just what I got more attention for. I was more recognized. In my four years playing basketball we won two games. That didn't give me a whole lot to be excited about for that sport.

Aly Wagner

I swam and I also played basketball, volleyball, and softball in grade school. Swimming was the one sport that I did on a club level. I think playing a lot of different sports as a child helped me because I became more well-rounded. It also helped me to meet other people socially, and then obviously I wasn't getting burnt out at a young age on one sport.

I quit swimming when I was 13 or 14. I think I always knew I'd choose to focus on soccer as my sport of choice. If there was a conflict between swimming and soccer, I'd choose soccer. I was never practicing swimming on my own, but I was always practicing soccer. There was never a point where I had to make a forced decision.

Did You Know?

Birgit Prinz was named German Player of the Year in 2001 and 2002.

Danielle Slaton

Other than soccer, I did ballet for a long time. I also ran track and played softball and volleyball. It probably wasn't until I was a sophomore or junior in high school that I slowly started to narrow things down. I stopped playing volleyball and softball when I was done with middle school, but I continued to run track in high school. Finally I decided that soccer was what I wanted to focus on, which was a decision that took longer for me to make than for some other people my age.

Lorrie Fair

If you are naturally good at something then you tend to gravitate towards it. In my case, I was a ball hog. I could dribble through people. I think it helped me. I learned to pass later. It's hard to teach dribbling after you've already learned to pass and pass and pass. So I was often yelled at by my team-mates. But I liked team sports because I liked having teammates, yet I could still affect the outcome of the game as an individual. There's this theme in soccer that you can't win without your team, yet you can change the game by yourself.

Hope Solo

These days girls quit everything around them and focus on that one sport that they hope to go far in. I believe you should play what you want to play. In high school, just don't play soccer—play volleyball AND soccer. A lot of people tried to force me to make that decision at a younger age than I really

Brandi Chastain

Cindy Parlow

had to. I see a lot of people doing it these days, and by the time they're a senior in high school, they're tired of that one sport. I think other sports just help balance things out. It helps your knowledge of sports in general. It helps your athleticism, but it also teaches you to to become more well-rounded.

 *When some of us were* playing soccer *in college and wondering what we would do after graduation, we couldn't even think of playing soccer as a real "job."*

We didn't know women would have that opportunity. We had to think about other kinds of careers that we might like.

 ### Nel Fettig

I really didn't have an athletic goal when I was growing up. I never really thought it was possible to say, "I'm going to be a professional athlete." My views were always toward doing something intellectual in a professional field or in medicine. I thought I wanted to be a doctor, always in the midst of any kind of tragedy trying to help out. It really wasn't until I got to college that I decided that medicine wasn't for me. I went to law school and tried to switch gears away from the science aspect into a little bit more of a thinking aspect. And then lo and behold, this league formed, and being a professional soccer player was suddenly a reality.

 ### Mia Hamm

I wanted to be a marine biologist until the movie *Jaws* came out and then that changed!

 ### Julie Foudy

I was going to be a doctor. After graduating from Stanford, I got accepted into their medical school, but I decided that I

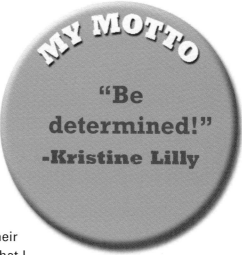

MY MOTTO

"Be determined!"
-Kristine Lilly

49

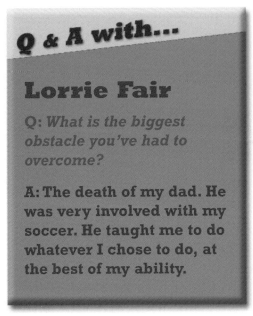

Q & A with...

Lorrie Fair

Q: *What is the biggest obstacle you've had to overcome?*

A: The death of my dad. He was very involved with my soccer. He taught me to do whatever I chose to do, at the best of my ability.

couldn't see myself having just one focus. It's not like law school where you can go into a lot of different areas. With medical school, you're limited to working with patients or doing research. That frightened me a little bit.

In hindsight, I wish I had gotten a law degree. I would have saved a lot of money with all the soccer contracts. There are a lot of things that go on that you have to deal with that involve contractual stuff, and that would have been great for the team. But also to have law as a base and a background would have been good.

Shannon MacMillan

I thought I was going to be a teacher. I was going to be a child development teacher because I just loved kids. I actually took the class taught by my high school's development teacher, and I was a teaching assistant for her. I told her I was going to come back to my little high school and take over her class. She's glad I'm playing soccer instead!

Kristine Lilly

I always wanted to be a veterinarian. But there's too much science to get involved in. So that changed. I didn't want to be a professional soccer player because I didn't know I would have that choice.

Cindy Parlow

I wanted to be a teacher like my mom. She teaches seventh grade at a Catholic school in Memphis. I wanted to teach kindergarten.

Aly Wagner

Danielle Slaton

Angela Hucles

I wanted to be many different things. One was a doctor, and I went to school thinking I was going to take pre-med classes. I tried psychology too. My mom is a psychologist. I didn't do too well in those classes, so I crossed that out. In the back of my mind I never really thought I would stop playing after college. So it's funny to think about that when at the time there wasn't any professional soccer.

 ## Danielle Slaton

I wanted to be a doctor. When I started college I took a bunch of pre-med classes, and that was my major. So if I weren't playing soccer I'd probably be in school right now.

 ## Carla Overbeck

I had a fifth grade teacher who took us to these volleyball tournaments. She would always say, "You're going to be on the Olympic volleyball team someday." I would watch the Olympics as a kid, and of course women's soccer was not in the Olympics, but I wanted to be a part of the Olympics because it was such a great thing. As I got older, soccer still was not in the Olympics, so I wanted to teach. I loved being around kids, and I enjoyed doing the soccer camps. I wanted to work in early childhood education because my sister and my mom were both teachers. I thought that was what I wanted to do—just to give something back to kids.

GROWING
WITH THE
GAME

*I felt that the only way
for me to push myself was to play
against better players.*

—Charmaine Hooper

TONY DiCICCO

Some girls play on boys teams, and playing against a boy's strength and speed can help improve your game. However, it's important to play in an environment where you can develop your own soccer personality. For example, Mia Hamm would not be able to dribble through players if she were playing Major League Soccer (MLS). She would have to try things. If she dribbled through players in MLS, the bigger and faster guys will strip her of the ball. She would just learn to pass it off. It's great for girls to train with boys, but you should also play with girls so that you develop the personality that will make you special.

Brandi Chastain

As a young girl what set me apart was my aggressive nature and the fact that I liked to be challenged and loved to compete. Those were the things that I think drove me as a young kid.

Julie Foudy

I grew up around a lot of South and Central American coaches who emphasized technical ability. Even with my first two coaches, with the team I played on for ten years (the Soccerettes), everything was about technique. So at an early age I was really lucky to get some good fundamental coaching on technical skills. For a player like me who doesn't have lightning speed, that was critical.

Briana Scurry

I was very athletic as a young player, and I was courageous. I just didn't fear anything. I was willing to dive for the ball at people's feet. It didn't really bother me. I was never afraid of getting kicked or anything like that. That's a huge part of goalkeeping, because if you are afraid of getting kicked you may as well just try something else. If you are athletic then you can become a very good goalkeeper. The ball is always bouncing around, and when a player shoots it, it can deflect, so you have to have the athletic ability to adjust to many situations.

Danielle Slaton

My speed has always been a strength. I'm not blazing fast like Olympic sprinter Marion Jones, but I have good speed. I also think my dedication and my coachability have helped me. It's important to not be shy and to speak up if you don't understand something. I think constantly having a dialogue and being open and respectful of my coaches has helped me a lot.

Carla Overbeck

I think my work ethic was my best trait. I remember one day I was going to practice for my club team, and my car broke down and my brother wouldn't give me a ride. So I put my ball in my backpack, and I ran to practice. Back then my club team would run two timed miles before every practice. They were very much into fitness. So my teammates drove by and they honked and waved while I was saying, "Pick me up! I'm not jogging for my health!"

Cindy Parlow

I would probably say my competitiveness was my greatest strength. It's hard to find girls at a young age who want to compete with other girls. A lot of times you see that they just want to be friends. They are afraid to tackle, or they don't want to upset a friend. I think I had a little bit of that, but I was more into winning. So it gave me a little bit of an edge where I was always competing whether it was my best friend or someone I didn't even know.

Did You Know?

In her spare time, **Kylie Bivens** likes to work on sculpture and woodworking.

Tiffany Roberts

I'd like to think that if you asked anyone what kind of player I am, they'd say, "Oh, she's one of the toughest players." I'm probably one of the smallest players in the WUSA, but I'm the most aggressive. I think it's from having three older brothers who were athletes that did karate and hockey. They used to try all their moves on me when I was growing up. So I was a little aggressive girl. I really went after the ball, and I was just a determined person.

Nel Fettig

I was able to pass the ball a little bit more precisely than some of my other friends. And when the ball would come to me, I'd be able to control it and dribble it every which way.

I never had great strength—I was a little runt, and I was always one of the slowest people out there—but I just tried to compensate for that in other ways. I don't think you can be the best in every aspect. You need to focus on your strengths, and obviously you need to develop your weaknesses as well. For me I think what worked was that I was able to control the ball without it getting away from me.

Tisha Venturini-Hoch

I understood the game. I could dribble and pass and run and do everything that anyone else could do. I was also very confident in my abilities. That's the most important thing— to stay confident and not get too down on yourself, or not let somebody tell you that you can't do something. I think that's a big part of growing up—being confident but not cocky and being a good team player.

Julie Foudy

I was always looking to improve. I think that's the first thing. You've got to *want* to improve. There's always another level that you can get to. For me what helped was learning from coaches, playing with different groups, and playing with guys. You have to be passionate about wanting to do better.

Brandi Chastain

Every time I went out onto the field was a chance for me to improve. Whether it was with my team or when I would come home from school on non-practice days, I'd probably spend two hours out on my front lawn just juggling the ball or kicking the ball against a wall. Every chance I got I would play soccer. I can't say I envisioned myself becoming a professional soccer player, but I knew that it was something that I really enjoyed doing. So I spent a lot of time doing it.

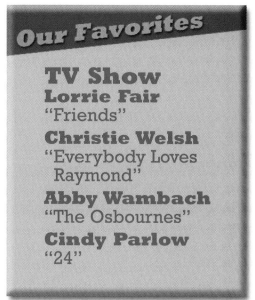

Our Favorites

TV Show
Lorrie Fair
"Friends"
Christie Welsh
"Everybody Loves Raymond"
Abby Wambach
"The Osbournes"
Cindy Parlow
"24"

Cindy Parlow

I think the one thing that truly made a difference for me was I always played against boys. I played on a girls club team but I would train with guys. I would train with their team or just go 1-v-1, 2-v-2—always playing against guys. They were bigger, faster, and stronger than me. I had to be creative and find new ways to beat them. And believe me, they aren't afraid to compete!

Abby Wambach

I played on a boys team from eleven to sixteen. And that taught me to play aggressively, how to go hard into a tackle. You have to play hard. And you have to play quick. I learned a lot from the boys I played with. They're all grown men now and probably don't realize how instrumental they were in my development as a soccer player.

 ## Charmaine Hooper

I wish when I was younger I had been able to play on boys teams because I just felt that when I was growing up I was always better than the other girls. When I got older I realized that being better than the other girls was not good enough. I felt that the only way for me to really push myself was to play against better players. When I left for college, I trained with guys for three months, and I improved more over those three months than I had my previous 18 years.

Leslie Gaston

I first played on a girls recreational team in Montgomery, Alabama. My two sisters and I all played on the same team and my mom was the coach. It wasn't really much of a challenge. Every year we won the championship. My mom approached me one day. She said, "Leslie, why don't you try out for the boys team?" I had another girl on my team who was willing to try out with me. So at first it was kind of nice because I had a friend there with me. Then my friend decided that she didn't want to continue, and it became more difficult. The hardest part was the socializing part of it. They were all young boys, so they really didn't like girls at that time. And they'd also make fun of me, and I never had a partner to train with. I always had to be the coach's partner.

Did You Know?

Jena Kluegel travels with a stuffed dog named Beacon.

There were different parts of it that were difficult, but I am very thankful that I had that experience because it made me a better player. It made me aggressive and more able to take on the physical challenges. I really think that it has helped my game—not only the skills but also the mental part of it. Just having to fight through bigger players and stronger players made a big difference.

Kristine Lilly

I would spend hours in the backyard juggling or playing soccer against my dog. Whenever I did something, like practice, I didn't goof off. I always gave 100% and worked hard.

Briana Scurry

I've always had the competitive edge, but I improved by going to soccer camp. I highly recommend—especially for girls trying to develop their skill—going to soccer camp at least once a year. For goalkeepers, you want a camp that integrates both goalkeeping and field play because you want the goaltending skills but you also need the field skills.

Breanna Boyd

There were two things I remember from the past where I think I improved the most. The first was when I got cut from a club team. I'd never been cut before in my life. So I went out every day after that, and I promised myself I would never get cut from a team like that again. My drive increased so much, and I became so much more determined. The second happened when I was fourteen. I tore the medial collateral ligament (MCL) in my knee. I really couldn't do anything athletic for the first four months of my recovery. The only thing I was allowed to do was get my foot on a ball. That's the first time where I really improved technically.

MY MOTTO

"Live every day like it's your last."

-Jenny Benson

Kristin Luckenbill

I think I improved from just being around better players. Also I've had some good goalkeeping coaches and have always had a good atmosphere to train in. But there's no better atmosphere than just getting out on the field and having the best players in the world shoot at you and try to beat you. I am so competitive that I don't like to get beat at anything! So it just makes me work even that much harder because I want to be better than them. I want to be the best.

Mary McVeigh

I improved because of competition in two ways. First, I always tried to get myself on the best teams that I could and compete with players who were better than me. The second is I competed with my older brother all the time. I always lost, but you can lose and still get better. That's how competition is.

Q & A with...

Jena Kluegel

Q: What's one of the funniest things about the people on your team?

A: Sometimes our international players pretend they don't understand us. We try to explain with body language, only to find out they understood us all along!

Joy Fawcett

I did a lot of practicing at home on my own. I was constantly dribbling a ball in front of my house or kicking it in the backyard or just playing with my brothers and sisters. I also improved by being willing to try new things and not being afraid to make mistakes. You might get a lot of different viewpoints from different coaches, and it's worth it to try to figure out what works for you.

TONY DiCICCO

The best thing you can do if you are a soccer player is to play the game as much as you can. Unfortunately, some people think that means playing 11-versus-11 with uniforms and referees. Most top athletes who play basketball probably started playing 2-on-2, or 3-on-3, or half court. Soccer players need to play one-on-one. It makes you stronger physically, and it tests your mental strength because when you are playing one-on-one and you're tired you're always wondering who's going to give up first. It also teaches you how to play defense, because you don't have anyone else to cover for you. You learn to attack because if you're going to score it's going to be totally up to you.

 ## Lorrie Fair
I used to kick the ball against the garage all the time... and broke a couple of windows.

Julie Foudy
I think the key is to become familiar with the ball by juggling, shooting, and dribbling. I can remember getting screamed at by my mom because I would break the garage door every other week.

Jenny Benson
I was a big fan of juggling. Juggling gets you touching the ball and gets you familiar with the ball. I would juggle at least an hour a day when I was younger. Just in the backyard with my dog. The dog would chase the ball, and we would have a blast together!

Mary McVeigh
I am a huge juggling fan. It was a competition thing. My best friend used to call at the end of every day, and we would tell each other our latest total. It improved my touch

Our Favorites

Books

Mia Hamm
The Giving Tree, by Shel Silverstein

Mary McVeigh
Harry Potter and the Sorcerer's Stone, by J.K. Rowling

Jennifer Grubb
To Kill a Mockingbird, by Harper Lee

Jennifer Tietjen-Prozzo
It's Not About the Bike: My Journey Back to Life, by Lance Armstrong

phenomenally. Juggling gives you not just physical skills, but also the confidence that you can make a ball do what you want. When a ball comes you will feel like you have control over it instead of it controlling you. That was both mentally and physically a huge, huge help for my game.

 ### Kylie Bivens

For me simple drills helped a lot. For example, during the first 40 minutes of practice we'd work on just bending balls. By doing real simple drills, everyone on our team was able to bend the ball with either side of their foot and hit it a good 35 or 40 yards.

 ### Tiffany Roberts

I'm a righty and I remember coaches saying to me that I had to do 100 left kicks a day. So my dad would go out there with me in the backyard, and I would practice using my left foot.

Shannon MacMillan

I loved doing anything around the goal. Whenever a coach said, "We're going to practice finishing your shooting," I said, "Yes, bring it on." Whether it was throwing balls, dribbling, or hitting a shot off the corner—anything around the goal got me fired up and excited.

Joy Fawcett

Christie Welsh

I just love anything with shooting, and I love doing volleys. I get somebody out there who can throw the ball out at me. Of course, a lot of my coaches won't say that's what I need to do most.

Nel Fettig

I always played 1-v-1 or 2-v-2 against the boys at school and against boys in my backyard. I think it can't help but make you a better player. Also attending soccer camps back then was a big thing. When I went to the Carolina Camp as a kid, we did dribbling skills exercises. That's something that kids can do on their own. You don't need space. You can do it inside. It's just quick footwork with the ball that really improves your touch and your ability to control the ball.

TONY DiCICCO

If you are only a right wing player, or a center back, you don't learn the game fully. You may be insecure or nervous about being moved to a different position. Learn to become a soccer player at many positions. At some point players are going to specialize, which is what they should do. But in the beginning you need to be open to all positions and learn as much you can.

Mia Hamm

I actually played midfield most of the time growing up. When you're young the coaches usually put the most skilled players at central midfield because they want you to be able to come back and get the ball and go forward with it as well. So I played center midfielder a lot until they moved me to forward when I was about fourteen.

Charmaine Hooper

I know a lot of kids today play different positions growing up, but I never did. However, I really wish that when I was younger I had been able to play a little bit of midfield and a little bit of defense. I think playing different positions helps you to get different experiences, and also helps you to better understand those positions and your responsibilities on the field.

Nel Fettig

It's funny. In high school I played midfield, but at higher levels like in the WUSA, I've always played defense. My coach for our Indiana State team decided to throw me in as a sweeper, which is the last defender before the goalkeeper. The regional coaches loved me playing there so much that when I played with the regional team I didn't play as a midfielder, I played as a defender. So in essence it was partly a decision made for me and partly because I truly enjoyed playing there.

I think my favorite position would be in the midfield because you are able to run up and down, but I don't think I'm as good in the midfield as I am in the back. It's good for you to recognize your strength and where you will best help the team.

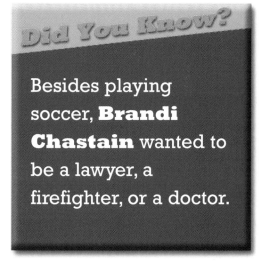

Did You Know?

Besides playing soccer, **Brandi Chastain** wanted to be a lawyer, a firefighter, or a doctor.

Carla Overbeck

I played all positions growing up. When I went to North Carolina, the coach basically said, "You know the whole defensive scheme. You need to play back there and just be a leader and a good communicator, and anchor the defense. And so that's the position that I was put into.

Briana Scurry

Breanna Boyd

For the most part I've always played defense. I always thought it was a challenge to shut down strikers. It's like a battle. I just came to love that battle, and I think there's no better feeling in the world than when you shut down the opposing strikers. I think defense is more of a mindset. It's just more about wanting to win and wanting to shut down the forwards.

Briana Scurry

From the time I was 16 on, I rarely got out of the goal. Nowadays most kids will try playing goal, and they don't like it. Back then there were no kids who wanted to try it, and since I was the only one willing to, I ended up being in there all the time. So that's how it happened. Like a tiger in a cage they closed the door on me and never let me out!

Our Favorites

Movies

Jennifer Tietjen-Prozzo – *Gladiator, Dumb and Dumber*

Lorrie Fair – *Crouching Tiger, Hidden Dragon*

Kylie Bivens – *Willy Wonka and the Chocolate Factory*

Leslie Gaston – *Shanghai Noon*

Kristin Luckenbill

I wasn't a goalkeeper until high school. Prior to that I played in the field. I liked scoring goals. When you are little, everyone plays in goal. Usually it's one of your best athletes who turns out to be a good goalkeeper. I just happened to naturally be a good athlete so they put me in goal, and then I ended up on a select team. We had another good goalkeeper, and the both of us switched off. We both played center, mid, forward, and in goal—then she quit. So that was it. I was the goalkeeper on that team.

Our Favorites

Pre-game Rituals

"I like to talk to each player on the team, even if it's just, 'come on' or 'let's go' or 'good luck.' I like to make contact with every teammate."

– Cindy Parlow

"I like to take a shower before games—I like to be clean before I get dirty! Plus, I use the time in the shower to set my goals for the game."

– Danielle Slaton

"I used to be very superstitious in college. I'm a little more level headed since then…now I juggle the ball 25 times before a game."

– Abby Wambach

"After everybody runs out and before the whistle blows, I touch the cross bar, kneel down, and say a prayer that I do the best I can and that everybody is safe."

–Briana Scurry

"I never change my cleats during a game. I did it once in my life and injured my knee. I'll never do that again!"

– Christie Pearce

 **Hope Solo**

Becoming a goalkeeper was the hardest decision for me as a player. I didn't play goal full-time until I hit college. All through high school I played on the field. Nobody from my hometown including my family had ever seen me play in goal. I could go 90 minutes without ever touching the ball, or I could get scored on three times and it was all my fault. It was tough.

I had every single person in my life come up to me saying,

Julie Foudy

"Are you going to play on the field again? You need to go out there and score goals, and you're not a goalkeeper." It was hard, and I think I overcame it with the help of my coaches at the University of Washington. They taught me more about the position and the mental side of the game. I think I had to overcome a lot of that before I played in goal. I studied the position. There was so much I didn't know about it, and I think that's why I didn't like it. I didn't respect it enough. Once I focused on playing in goal, positive things started happening.

Mary McVeigh

I have always played center mid purely because I like to be in the middle of things. You always have to be conscious of what's going on around you and always have the opportunity to make yourself part of the play. Everything you do is very relevant—you can make an impact at every moment when you play in the middle of things, and that's always what intrigued me about the position. Something else you get from playing in the middle is you have to be part of everything that everybody is doing. So, for example, I played point guard in basketball and always had to know not only what play someone was running but also what everybody else was supposed to be doing during that play. That's kind of how I am in soccer. I try to make it a point to understand every position.

Shannon MacMillan

I think it's extremely important to experience playing all the positions. If you don't try the positions, you're not going to find out what naturally is your best spot out there. If you're a well-rounded player, you also give your coach some additional options. If someone goes down and you need to step in and fill another role, the more positions you can play the more likely the coach will keep you around.

TEAMS
AND
TRAVELS

I've been in places that I otherwise wouldn't have gone... and that's been a really cool thing.

—Christie Welsh

TONY DiCICCO

There are advantages and disadvantages to playing on club teams. You get a coach who's played the game and is a professional, so he or she will be a great teacher and look to develop you as a person, not just as a soccer player. It allows you to play with and against better players so you are going to develop more quickly. One of the negatives is that you can burn out. You go to tournaments every weekend, and when you are playing four to six games in a weekend, after a while that isn't fun anymore. I call it "tournamentitis" where so many clubs take their teams to so many tournaments. Think hard about what you want to do with soccer, and talk to your parents about it.

 *When girls first started playing soccer, it was tough to find a team. Like we've said, some of us started on boys teams. Sometimes it depended on which city we were from. The Olympic development program offered some of us a great opportunity to get good coaching and to play against girls who were bigger and stronger. Being challenged like that can make you a better player.*

Mia Hamm

I competed on boys teams growing up. That was pretty much all we had. Other than briefly when I was 10, I didn't play on an all girls team until I was 14.

Kristine Lilly

I played on boys teams until I entered high school. They didn't have a freshman girls team. They only had junior varsity girls or a freshman boys team. My parents were going to fight to allow me to play with the freshman boys team, but I ended up making the girls varsity my freshman year.

Carrie Moore

I played on boys teams. There wasn't even a thought of a girls team until I was in eighth grade. I was the only girl on the boys team for a little while. Even the first year that there was a girls team in Roanoke, I played both on the girls team and the boys team because the girls team was awful. We didn't score our first goal until December.

Danielle Slaton

When I was five I started playing YMCA soccer on all-boys teams because there were no all-girls teams when I was growing up. But I don't really think playing with boys made a huge impact because we were were just five, six, and seven years old. We were basically the same physically at that age. I think that young girls play-ing with boys who are maybe a little bit older— when boys are starting to get a little faster and aggressive—that might have more of an impact.

Briana Scurry loves her two Labrador Retrievers—a yellow female named "Blockheed," and a chocolate-colored male named "Shaniq."

Carla Overbeck

I came from Dallas, a big metropolitan area that had tons of girls teams that were very competitive. Our club team was one of the better ones, and so every team would want to go after us and beat us. And so we had a very, very competitive league. I did-n't have to be on boys teams like Mia Hamm and Kristine Lilly did. So I was kind of fortunate that way.

Tiffeny Milbrett

I never had to play with boys because there were always girls teams. I give Oregon so much credit. I always felt like Oregon was ahead of the times in offering sports for women and girls.

Our Favorites

Pre-game Foods

Mia Hamm – Peanut butter and jelly sandwich

Tiffany Roberts – Banana, peanut butter, and honey sandwich

Marinette Pichon – Pasta, Chicken

Jennifer Tietjen-Prozzo - Pancakes

Angela Hucles

When I first started playing competitively with a travel team, it was with boys. This is a testament to how much the sport has grown. There weren't really very many competitive girls teams when I was growing up.

I think the Olympic development program (ODP) really helped. With that program I was able to travel and play against other girls from around the country. It was like a mini version of trying out for the national team. I finally met people who were like me in terms of the dedication to the sport and the sacrifice that we had to make. We did so much traveling, and we missed so many different things from high school or junior high. I think it was nice to finally be around other girls who were similar to me. I think that helped me enjoy the sport even more and not feel different than other people. We got to share the passion for the game. We traveled during the weekends and went to camps away from our families. It gave us all the opportunity to play against top competition for our age group in the state, the region, and then nationally.

Joy Fawcett

I think the Olympic development program was a huge benefit for me because of the input from coaches. I think my youth coaches were good to an extent, but they didn't know the game all that well. With ODP you always had different coaches on different teams at different levels with various viewpoints. So that was good, and it was competitive. You're playing against girls who are as good as you or better, and that makes you a better player.

Katia

Nel Fettig

Kids today are so lucky that they are able to play all year round at the highest level. At the time I was growing up, I'd go try out for the Olympic development program for four days, make the team, and then go play at Thanksgiving for a week. That was the only time we had for playing at the highest level.

Aly Wagner

I think that the soccer clubs have great training from the top down. They've developed players along the way so they know what it takes. And there's obviously precedence within the club of how they're going to have their players grow. So I would say clubs are a good way to go.

Mary McVeigh

My dad found out about the Olympic development program when I was ten. My brother was older, so he was the right age to try out, but luckily my dad took me anyway. So when I was ten I made the Massachusetts ODP teams—the under-12 teams which gave me a chance to play with older girls. I wasn't very big, and I wasn't very strong, but I think from there it took off. I started to get to know people in eastern Massachusetts which was a big help because western Massachusetts is not really the mecca of soccer in the state. It's really Boston. So getting to know people from Boston helped me in eventually joining the Boston Bolts.

Did You Know?

After she married, superstition encouraged **Jennifer Tietjen-Prozzo** to keep Tietjen as her last name for the 2002 season, but she finally changed that to Tietjen-Prozzo for 2003.

TONY DiCICCO

A coach has the tough job of telling players that not everyone is going to make the team. That's reality. It's a very painful thing. It's not an attack on the player as a person. Whether a player makes the team or not is determined by the impression her playing makes on the coach. If this happens to you, the best way to handle it is to think, "I didn't impress that coach as much as I needed to." Ask yourself, "What do I need to do to make sure that never happens again," and work on that. That's an example of a good attitude that can make you a better player.

We're so glad there are now more and more opportunities for girls to play soccer. But because girls soccer is now so popular, there can be a lot of pressure on you and a lot of competition when you try out for the top club and traveling teams.

Joy Fawcett

My freshman year in high school my coach dragged me to a club tryout. I was really shy so my coach said, "You are going to go try out." She made me go. I didn't know anyone because no one in my area tried out. I think my sister went with me just to be nice. But it was just a lot of girls, and everyone was pretty nervous including me. I remember doing a lot of technical stuff, just so they could see my level. My confidence was not very strong. That's one thing that I've always struggled with. Because I wasn't confident, I never felt content with what I had done. I always wanted to get better, so I always continued to work hard at it.

Breanna Boyd

At every level there are always tryouts, and usually there are three rounds of tryouts. At the tryouts, I would always match myself up against the best forward on the other team. I always believed in being really aggressive in tryouts.

Leslie Gaston

I had to try out for my Olympic development team. I always get extremely nervous before anything, including games. The same thing with tryouts. I just tell myself I'll give 100% and I'll try my best, play my hardest, and that's all I can do. There isn't really any special thing that I do. You just have to be confident in your abilities. I think the hardest thing for me—and part of the reason why I got so nervous and I still do—is sometimes I doubt myself. I shouldn't do it, but it actually makes me play that much harder.

Mary McVeigh

I know that a lot of girls go to tryouts and try to be the flashiest player there. They are told to do something that makes them stand out. That usually works, but I found out that didn't work for me. The more I tried to stand out, the more I opened myself up to feel like I blew it if I messed up one time. That really affects your tryout. My advice would be to do all the little things right. That's what I focused on. Every touch or easy play that came to me I made sure that I did it right. So there was nothing that anybody could say about me that meant I couldn't play—nothing stood out that I was doing wrong. It's like, if you can be consistent and you can just play calmly and play simply, I personally think that's the way to go in a tryout.

Tryouts are all about trying to impress a coach with your abilities— both your soccer skills and your leadership skills—while feeling the pressure of trying to make a team. We all know what this feels like and have some advice for impressing a college coach or a national team coach.

Joy Fawcett

The biggest thing is making sure you're seen. There're so many players in the United States, and it's hard for college coaches to see everyone. So you need to make sure that you're being seen. If it's a traveling team that goes to the big tournaments that college coaches go to, then that's where you need to

Shannon
MacMillan

be. If it's the Olympic development team where you're going to be seen, then I would do that.

Breanna Boyd

As a defender, you're not going to be flashy, so I don't think it was a game where I was first noticed. My first provincial team coach really believed in me. She told me, "One day you're going to be on the national team," and told other people to look out for me. For me that meant a lot because as a defender you're not really going to get noticed any other way unless you're really offensive-minded. I was always a defensive defender.

Our Favorites

Hobbies

Mia Hamm
Golf, cooking

Carrie Moore
Playing chess, needlepoint

Tiffany Roberts
Burning cd's, shopping

Marinette Pichon
Watching baseball

Once you make the team, be ready for practice, more practice…and did we mention practice?! There can be a lot of travel involved too, so be prepared.

Christie Welsh

During the fall I played high school ball where we would practice every weekday. My club team would also practice on the weekend if we could fit it in. But in the spring we would practice twice a week with the club team, and then if you played on the Olympic development team you'd have practice once or twice a week with them. So basically I'd practice for four days a week and then have a game on the weekend.

Breanna Boyd

I probably practiced every day—sometimes twice a day. I was always on at least two soccer teams. I'd even play soccer at my school where we'd have soccer practice or games after school. Sometimes I'd have two practices or games in one night.

Deliah Arrington

After school my mom would pick me up after she got off from work. We'd drive about an hour for practice and then practice for however long, and on the way back I'd do my homework in the car. I practiced maybe twice a week, and then I was there every weekend. So I went back and forth maybe three times a week.

Mary McVeigh

I usually had two club practices a week and two Olympic development practices a week. My club practices were about 45 minutes away. For my ODP team I had to travel from western Massachusetts to Boston for practice. Those were Wednesday and Saturday. So I had to give up my entire Saturday and give up my entire Wednesday night.

Aly Wagner

When I started getting really competitive, I still only trained three times a week, usually two hours at a time. It's different now. I think it's a lot more intense now than it was when I was

Most Embarrassing Moment

"I was running to the restroom right before halftime. I stepped on one of the legs of my sweatpants...then fell...and tore my pants right on the field in front of thousands of people!"

—**Breanna Boyd**

Charmaine Hooper

growing up, which is hard to believe. I know that kids are training every day now. It just seems so absurd to me how hard these kids are pushing themselves. I think there's going to be a lot of kids who suffer from burnout.

Brandi Chastain

I think we had two practices a week, and they were pretty rudimentary as far as fundamentals were concerned. We were all learning the game together for the first time. We did a lot of running and jumping jacks and sit ups, and we hated it, but it was good for us. We also played a lot. We would make boundaries, put the ball down, and just play.

Traveling to play for us was like an hour drive. That became the big trip. And back in those days when you traveled for a tournament you'd stay with the host team's families. You wouldn't stay in a hotel or anything like that. It was kind of nice because when we hosted a tournament we'd reciprocate, and those teams would stay with our families. So it was more of a family-like environment than it is now. I didn't go to a regional tournament until my last year of under-17 when we went to Washington state. So it wasn't quite as much of a struggle as it is today.

Cindy Parlow

I think some of my fondest memories are actually the journeys to the tournaments, not so much the tournaments themselves. My parents were very involved in my life growing up with soccer. They traveled everywhere we went. My parents had a big van. Seven, eight, sometimes up to 10 girls would pile into the van. We would travel from my home in Memphis, Tennessee to places like Jackson (Mississippi), Nashville, or Atlanta. The camaraderie of those trips and eating tons of candy on the way down—those are the things that I remember the most.

Aly Wagner

Around the time I was 11 or 12 we got pretty competitive and started traveling from San Jose, California to Southern California and Arizona. We loved going to hotels—just running around the halls and kicking the balls into doors. We got into so much trouble as kids. You had your best friends with you, so it was like a giant sleepover.

Breanna Boyd

I started traveling from my home in Calgary, Canada when I was 12. The select team would go to places like Arizona and California once or twice a year. I think it was all about having fun back then—just going out with your team and going to new places. I don't have any bad memories about traveling.

Leslie Gaston

I traveled every weekend from Montgomery, Alabama to Birmingham. It was an hour and a half trip every weekend. I traveled with both boys and girls teams. They were always a lot of fun—especially the girls team—because my teammates became my best friends. The difficult part was missing a lot of the fun stuff in high school. Parties were only on the weekends, so I really couldn't do any of that. I had to miss my homecoming and prom and a lot of things that high school kids enjoy. But I definitely think it was worth it.

Christie Welsh

When I was 13 I was on the under-14 regional team, and the first place I traveled to by myself was Florida. That is a long way from Long Island, New York! In the beginning, I think I took traveling for granted. The biggest thing to me was playing soccer. I didn't really enjoy the places we would visit. As I've grown and re-visited all those places, I've been able to take in the different cultures and enjoy the surroundings. It's been a learning process over time—not to just take these trips to play soccer but to absorb what was going on around me as well. I've been in places that I otherwise wouldn't have gone and my parents could only dream of going to, and that's been a really cool thing.

Mary McVeigh

I think for a young girl the best part of traveling is you get to stay in hotels with your best friends and go out to eat. When I was 12 my Northhampton, Massachusetts club team went to three regional tournaments. We won Massachusetts, so we went to New Jersey. When I was fourteen I got to go to Niagara Falls. It just kept getting better, like the Florida tournament we went to. When you start to hit high school all the tournaments become purposeful. You need to go because of college or you need to get seen, and that's a little different from when you're younger and going just to have a great time.

Hope Solo

I'm from a little town in Washington state called Richland. When I was 12, all the teams were over in Seattle on the west side of the state. So every Saturday and Sunday morning we had a four hour drive to Seattle, which was big for a bunch of 12-year-olds.

When I was younger I liked piling into a car with my friends. We'd have games to play. But as I got older, it got pretty tedious. It was a big struggle trying to balance being a normal teenager or a normal college student versus being a high profile athlete. I wanted the best of both worlds, and I've only recently come to learn that if I wanted to be on the national team, if I want-

Kristine Lilly

ed to be the best I could be, then I needed to make soccer my life. At first I wouldn't let soccer define me as a person or really take over my life. That's a struggle you must overcome to become a top soccer player.

 ## Angela Hucles

I would say if you enjoy all the traveling then keep it up. And if it's something that you think is helping your development, why not? It's a great experience. It's not just the soccer at that age. You'll have so many different experiences and memories when you do this type of stuff—friends that you'll make. If you're not enjoying it then that's when you need to evaluate what's going on because it can keep you from doing other great things. I do think that if you are interested in pursuing college soccer, there are a lot of college scouts who will go to these types of tournaments. So that's an added bonus when you become involved with teams that travel.

DEALING WITH OBSTACLES

Setbacks are always going to be emotional things. I've never gotten too wound up in roadblocks, because I believe something good is going to come of them.

—Breanna Boyd

 **For an athlete** *there are numerous obstacles that can get in the way of "success." The women of the WUSA have dealt with all kinds of setbacks on the way to playing soccer at the highest level. Injuries, lack of confidence, time commitments—you name it, we've been there. No matter what form the obstacles took, we all had a recipe to overcome them.*

Brandi Chastain

The first real hurdle came my way in junior high school. That's when they had a team with only boys. It was co-ed but no girls went out for it. I wanted to be on that team, but that was the first time that a coach said to me, "You can't play because you're a girl." It was as shocking to me as it was to the boys I grew up with who knew I could play. "Why can't she be on the team?" they said.

Q & A with...

Katia

Q: *What is one of your best soccer memories?*

A: Scoring against Germany in the first round of the 1999 Women's World Cup.

I was mad and wasn't going to take no for an answer, so I worked really hard to gain the confidence of the coach. I also had earned the respect of the boys, and they supported me. It meant so much to me when a group of them went to the coach and said, "Give her a chance, and she'll show you that she can do what it is that the team needs."

My mom always told me never to give up on something that I was interested in. I've seen that junior high coach a few times since then, and he remembers that I never gave up.

Brandi Chastain

Briana Scurry

There were four of us who came up through the club team ranks and had played together for years. In ninth grade, we were still part of the junior high, but we were as good, if not better, than, a lot of those players in high school. We could've hung with them, and we felt we could have made the team better. However, the school had a policy where you couldn't play on a high school team sport if you were in ninth grade. We petitioned the city of Anoka, Minnesota, to be allowed to play.

I remember going to court to petition. The court was saying, "You are not developed enough in ninth grade to play." We obviously thought we were. It helped our cause that the high school team hadn't won a game in two years, so they couldn't do any worse with us on the team. As a compromise, they told us that three of us could play. The first year we won five games. The next year nine, then eleven, and in my senior year we won the state tournament!

Tiffany Roberts

When I was really young I think that coaches were turned off by me because I was really small compared to everyone else. They glanced at me and said, "This girl can't play on my team. She's too little. She'll get pushed around." But as soon as I went and tried out, I changed their minds right away.

Often making the team is based on a tryout. Sometimes you want badly to make the team, and then the word comes you're cut. Almost no one is immune to the process. The important thing is how you deal with the disappointment.

Shannon MacMillan

Right after I finished my collegiate season in 1995, I got cut from the Olympic team. Tony DiCicco picked 24 people to go into residency in Florida, and here I was coming off of my senior season. I had won all the college awards, the MAC, the Hermann. I was going in with the most confidence I ever had as a player, and he said, "Sorry."

I remember going back to Clive Charles, my coach at the University of Portland, and crying about how unfair the world was. Clive said, "You'll get your chance." He said, "You have 24 hours to mope, then you have to be ready."

MY MOTTO

"Dream big and believe in yourself!"
-Shannon MacMillan

Three weeks later the veterans held out on a contract dispute, and they needed to fill a roster spot. So I got the call. And from there I worked my way in and then all the way up to being a starter and leading scorer in the '96 Olympics.

I've also had injuries. I had a screw put in my foot and had knee surgery. There are always roadblocks, but it's because of those roadblocks that I've had to work that much harder. I learned you can't take anything for granted.

Mary McVeigh

When I was 16 I was cut from the Olympic development team. I had reached a point where I expected to make it, which is a terrible thing to do. I had not focused on the simple things. I would mess up and tell myself it was okay. I didn't have that self-motivation to say that every touch matters. I was off the team and knew it was my fault.

I asked the coach for another chance, so he invited me to indoor practices. We were having 1-v-1 tournaments with 27 people. He told us, "The top 11 players make my team, and most of them tend to be my starters." Those were the stakes. Every touch counted. I ended up winning the tournament so he let me back on the team, and that was huge. The whole process was not only a wake up call but just inspiration for me to know that every tryout matters no matter how sure you are that you will make the team.

TONY DiCICCO

If you injure yourself playing soccer, it's okay to feel bad, it's okay to feel sorry for yourself, but don't let that take over how you're going to get back to being a top player. It's a tragedy, but it's not catastrophic, and you can overcome it. Often when players are injured, they come back stronger because they become used to weight training as part of their overall training. This can make them a better player. Brandi Chastain overcame injury, becoming an Olympic gold medalist and a World Cup champion. You can do it, too.

Leslie Gaston

Everybody says there's a silver lining to every cloud. I've been riddled with injuries ever since seventh grade. I have had five anterior cruciate ligament (ACL) surgeries and six other knee surgeries. I've broken my leg in half, I've broken my collarbone and broken my nose and my ankle twice each. I've even been hospitalized with a kidney ailment for a week.

I didn't understand why this kept happening to me. I would follow the protocol for the rehabilitation, and I wouldn't start playing too soon or anything. I would feel ready, but the doctor would say I still had to wait, so it was

Did You Know?

Leslie Gaston has undergone 11 different knee surgeries throughout her soccer career.

really frustrating. I don't think that I would have been able to do it without the support system that I had, especially the coaches, trainers, and medical staff at the University of North Carolina. They never once let me feel discouraged.

I feel I'm a pro at rehab now. But after going through all of these various things I realized that I have to listen to my body. I now take everything very slowly, trying to watch my body and figure out what it's telling me.

Aly Wagner

Coming back from serious injury is extremely hard. I've told so many people I'd rather run fitness every day than have to go to therapy again for an ACL because it's excruciating—it's amazingly hard work. It's hard to see that it's paying off at the time, and it's also very painful.

MY MOTTO

"Try to understand people, not judge them."

-Briana Scurry

Mentally, I would say that it's something you can't really take to heart. You just have to believe in yourself and know that you can come back from it. In order to get over that hurdle you must think about the long run, why you're doing it, and how much you want to get back out on the field because you love the game.

Joy Fawcett

I think the toughest thing when you have an injury is being away from the team. You feel left out. You don't feel a part of the team, and you start telling yourself that they might not need you. It's important to make sure that you rehab hard and get it done. It's hard work. I think rehab is harder than actually playing the game.

But it gives you that hunger and that desire to get better because the whole time you're away you want to get back. You see what you're missing. That perspective can help you a lot when you return.

Breanna Boyd

When I was 14, I tore the MCL in my knee. At first I was incredibly disheartened by the injury, but it ended up being a blessing in disguise because I really had to take time to work on my technical skills. That's all I could do.

Setbacks are always going to be emotional things. You're not going to feel great about them, but I've always thought that things happen for a reason. So as much as I let events like that drive me, I've never gotten too wound up in roadblocks, no matter what it is, because I believe something good is going to come of them.

Mia Hamm

I've been pretty lucky, and it's only been the past two or three years that I've had to deal with injuries. You have to first prepare yourself mentally for dealing with it. I think that's the hardest part—psychologically pushing yourself through

Carla Overbeck

those tough days when you feel that you're not getting any better. You don't see the improvements that you want to see. But by sticking to your rehab you will get back.

Carla Overbeck

I experienced an illness before the Sydney Olympics. I contracted Graves Disease, which is a thyroid problem, and did radiation treatment for that. Then I had knee surgery right after that so I was a member of the Olympic team but didn't get to play. That was difficult for me, but my whole attitude was that I was in a team sport. I knew I couldn't contribute on the field; however, I knew I could contribute off the field and from the sidelines. I was the captain of that team, and to be on the bench during games obviously was difficult. But I continued to have a voice and tried to lead as best I could from the bench. That's just what I had to do.

You're going to be dealt unfortunate situations in your life, and you need to stay positive and realize that, yes, it is a team sport. The things that you brought to that team before can still apply even though you're injured. You might not be able to do it on the field, but you'll be there at practice or you'll be there from the sidelines and you can still be a good soldier. That's what being a part of a team is all about.

Angela Hucles

An injury can be devastating, and fortunately I have not had to go through it, but I've seen friends go through it. It's one of those things where I've been so amazed by people. They just keep pushing on. I think the way that they've been successful in life has been what's helped them get through their injury and stick to the program. I suggest not trying to accomplish everything right away but realizing that it's going to be a process—making sure that you are not being overwhelmed with things but having faith in yourself that you'll get through it.

Cindy Parlow

I've been pretty fortunate. I have only been cut once and I haven't had any serious injuries. I've had little injuries along the way, but that's kind of an occupational hazard.

WUSA GIRL'S GUIDE TO SOCCER LIFE

I think Brandi Chastain and Shannon MacMillian are great examples of overcoming obstacles. Both players had been cut from the national team and look at them now. They're back, and they are stars for the team. I think their persistence and motivation to play the game that they love has been outstanding, and I think you can see that from a lot of different players. They might have been cut, or they might have had an injury or maybe something else has gone on in their life where they took a step back from soccer. I think the best advice that I could give anyone is to find your true passion in life. Whether it's soccer, another sport, science, business...whatever—find out what your passion is and do that. Life is too short.

BALANCING ACT

*It's hard trying to decide what
things to sacrifice for soccer...
There's more to life than
just one interest.*

—Danielle Slaton

TONY DiCICCO

We now have soccer athletes who are moving away from home at age 15, 16, and 17 and going to soccer specific high schools where they go to school but soccer is part of their everyday curriculum. Those kids eat, live, and breathe soccer, so they have great talent for it, but they still have to be careful that soccer is not their entire life. It's important to have other skills and interests so you'll be prepared for the day when soccer is not your main focus.

Every athlete who's a student has a hard time balancing school and her sport. It can be difficult juggling homework with practices. At each level of soccer and school there are more demands on your time. Making a plan and adjusting it as you grow older is very important. Most parents understand the importance of getting an education and having different interests, and chances are your parents understand how important your sport is to you. Your mom and dad may be able to teach you effective ways to balance your life. It may not feel like it right now, but it is possible to have a full life outside of soccer! You don't want your life to be consumed with just soccer and schoolwork.

Melissa Moore

When I was in elementary school, I would have to go home and do my homework before I could go out and play. A lot of times you had time after school before soccer practice, and you'd try to get it all done before practice. In high school it was the same thing. My parents were also a part of it too because if I fell below a certain grade point average soccer would be taken away until I raised my grades. You have to try to get your homework done and study for tests before you go out and play. A lot of times that's not realistic because you have practice right after school, but then once practice is over you have to go home and get your work done.

Tiffany Roberts

I took school very seriously growing up, and my parents really made sure that school was a priority in my life. They always told me that school was number one, so in my mind that's what I grew up hearing all the time. Although I'd travel to play games, I still would have to take my schoolwork with me. To me, if I got good grades and I did well in school it would be easier for teachers to let me go early to play games. I also hoped they would be more lenient with my homework and not give me as much because they knew I was a responsible student. I figured if I have a bad attitude and don't get good grades how are these teachers going to let me go overseas and play with the U.S. team? So I took it very seriously.

Did You Know?

Charmaine Hooper can speak Japanese! She practices sometimes with Homare Sawa.

# Joy Fawcett

You won't be able to play soccer if you don't do the schoolwork. So you've got to make sure you put the effort into school. You might end up giving up other things like going out with your friends, but make sure that you get the school-work done first. If you don't do well now, you don't get to play in high school which means you won't get to play in college. College is where you're going to be seen by scouts, and you don't want to lose your chance to excel on the next level.

Abby Wambach

For me, balancing academics and soccer was imperative. It was important to my family that I do well in school first and then do well in sports. But early on, you could tell I was going to be a better athlete than I was going to be a student. I think my parents knew that. I always tried very hard, but I was never an

A student. My first love was soccer, and that's kind of the attitude I had. I was a B or C student. I just did what I needed to get by, which is *not* the way to go. At this point I regret it. I wish I had done better in school.

Tisha Venturini-Hoch

It was tough for me growing up. I wasn't the smartest kid on the block. I didn't like to spend a lot of time studying. I was very active, and I wanted to do a million other things. Academics didn't come easy for me, but I knew I had to do it so I was very disciplined. I tried to do extra work and really work hard on my academics. My dad was a smart guy. So he was my tutor. Even in college I'd come home, and he'd go on the road with our team. He would tutor four or five of us on anatomy. It was tough for me, and I had to have a lot of help. If you don't get those good study habits when you are young then it is really tough to ever get them. In high school, there's so much going on, and if you're not disciplined and balanced early, it just gets harder and harder. I think when you get to college if you are not already on the right track you are in real trouble.

Danielle Slaton

As I was growing up, youth soccer was exploding so much that you had your club team, you had your high school team, and you had the Olympic development program. There was also the youth national team. All of them wanted a little bit of my time. Meanwhile I had schoolwork, my friends, and family. I tried to have something of a social life. That was really hard. I definitely had to sacrifice for soccer. I remember missing the prom. I was devastated. One of the hardest things for me was just learning to find a balance in my life. It's hard trying to decide what things to sacrifice for soccer and what soccer things to give up to get a balanced life. There is more to life than just one interest. Looking back I learned to manage my time by prioritizing things. I know there are more young players facing this challenge than ever before. The sooner you can work on managing time and get help doing that, the less stressful your life will be.

Shannon MacMillan

If you don't do well in school, you are not going to be able to play soccer. I had to be more disciplined because of soccer because I knew while other people were going out on weekends I had to be in bed early because I had a game the next day. I would use road trips—every flight, every hour in the airport—to catch up on my studies. For me, because soccer was paying for my education, I was going to take full advantage of it. If you're not disciplined already, start right away. Learn how to schedule your time, and all aspects of your life will improve.

Charmaine Hooper

In high school it was not too hard to balance both because my parents were pretty strict. They were both teachers, so I was not allowed to watch much TV. At about four o'clock, the TV went off and we had to do homework. If we didn't have homework, we had to get a book and read or they made work up for us. I was able to balance school and soccer by playing in the afternoon and always doing my homework at night.

Julie Foudy

I was always really disciplined about my studies. I knew that I wanted a good education and I wanted to go to a good college. I don't know if that decision came from my competitive drive or my parents, but I always was really conscious of that. I took school very seriously and did really well in school. I knew that if I couldn't play soccer, I'd always have my education.

Our Favorites

Music

Hope Solo
Madonna

Abby Wambach
Dave Matthews Band

Jenny Benson
KISS

Kristine Lilly
Third Eye Blind

Lorrie Fair
Boyz II Men

Breanna Boyd

Athletics aren't as highly regarded in Canada as they are in the United States. I never got any sympathy or understanding from the academic world. I had to learn how to communicate and work with my teachers. They were definitely not that understanding of the importance of athletics when I was growing up. I think that trying to balance academics and an athletic career can prove difficult at times. I wanted to do well at both, so sometimes I had to make sacrifices in one or the other.

Kristin Luckenbill

I think it's absolutely necessary to balance not just academics and athletics but also other things that may interest you. A lot of times when I met the new kids that were joining my team, I thought it was a negative that some of them were just soccer, soccer, soccer. I thought that even though they might be great soccer players they were too into just doing one thing. I really like people who are a little more well rounded. I think it's good in life if you have a lot of different things going on.

Danielle Slaton

The one thing that I've learned over the years is that it's okay to say no. It's okay if someone calls you and says we really need you to come to this camp or we really need you to do this project and you say, "Look, I'm sorry but I really have too much on my plate," or "I'll be there next time if I can." Set out a plan, whether it be for that day or that week or the next month or the entire semester. Plan things out and look ahead so you can see where you have a more difficult schedule or you can see where you can take time out and go on a vacation. Planning ahead with a schedule definitely helps me.

Nel Fettig

Academics and school were extremely important to me. I excelled in the classroom and had a career path in mind. How I balanced school and soccer is that I've always been a firm believer in time management and being focused. It's okay to lose your focus. I don't think you can be focused 100% of the time or you are not going to be enjoying life. I think you should be focused for the entire practice or focused for the hour and a half it takes to do schoolwork. Then you might leave yourself with an hour and a half to talk to your friends. I think that's what it takes. If you dilly-dally at practice it may end up being an hour and 45 minutes, where if you just

Did You Know?

Lorrie Fair has an identical twin sister, Ronnie, who also plays in the WUSA with the San Diego Spirit.

stayed focused you would be in and out in an hour. In school I also made sure that I would always make a to-do list. As I got things done I would cross them off. If I didn't get something done it would carry over, and it would be the first thing on my list the next day. I'm a believer in lists, whether you write it out or it's a checklist in your mind.

Kylie Bivens

I missed out on a lot of parties and stuff. I know that sounds kind of ridiculous now, but I did miss out. I missed out on boyfriends. There wasn't much time for anything else other than soccer and school. There were times I got called in for under-21 national team stuff, and I decided I didn't want to do it. I was a little burnt out. I was playing year round and didn't know how to balance all of it and make it all work. That's just growing up.

Jennifer Tietjen-Prozzo

In junior high and high school, I played two or three sports. I played basketball and volleyball as well as soccer. I always made sure I had a study hall period to catch up on schoolwork. Then in college, I actually found it easier when I was in season because there are plenty of practices and plenty of games, and you know you only have a certain amount of time you can study. So for me it's better when you have a set schedule.

Briana Scurry

It's a difficult balance between academics and athletics. But I found in college it was actually easier for me to organize my time in the fall when the soccer season was full tilt. I had a little bit lighter course load in the spring and less soccer. In the fall, I had certain set times that I had to do my homework. After class I'd eat, go to training, eat, rest, do homework, hang out, sleep. Same thing every day of the week. That worked really well because I knew what I had to get done. In the spring I didn't have as much soccer. I had practice two or three times a week. I noticed it was a lot harder for me to organize when I was going to do my work because I had all day to do it. I'd do some, and then something else more appealing would pop up, and I might get sidetracked. So I realized that having that regimented schedule in the fall actually made it easier. Time management is very important but it's up to you to do it.

Carla Overbeck

You definitely have to learn to balance and manage your time. When you know you have a practice, you have to get your work done and be efficient in doing that before practice. It's also important to use your time wisely after practice. In the spring, it was a little bit more relaxed as far as soccer was concerned. So sometimes your work would just kind of get away from you because you had too much time to do it. Now as a coach at Duke, I realize how important academics are because even though soccer is a great thing, at some point it's going to end. You need to fall back on an education to bring you through the rest of your life.

Lorrie Fair

Growing up it was a rule that I couldn't do anything until I finished my homework. So it was an easy decision for me. I'm also lucky in that I don't need a lot of sleep. In college I never missed a class until my senior year. I would always go to my eight o'clock class even if I had been out the night before.

Aly Wagner

Jennifer Grubb

Playing soccer is like having a full-time job while you are a full-time student. It becomes a twelve-hour day, at least. You've got four or five hours a day of your sport and then classes, and you have to make time for homework and meetings. Obviously you need to be good at time management. So you just have to figure out what needs to be done and in what order and what gets top priority.

TONY DiCICCO

Currently we are seeing kids drop out of soccer in large numbers once they reach 16. There are reasons for this. By that age, most kids will find things that interest them other than soccer, such as dating or playing other sports. There's nothing wrong with that, but often new interests make it difficult to keep up with the demands of soccer. Many kids feel the pressure from coaches and parents to make soccer the top priority. They don't understand how to work soccer into other parts of their life, so they think they have to drop it completely.

If you feel you're burning out on soccer and want to try other activities, talk to your coach and your parents about your schedule. They should be able to help you figure out the times in the year when you will be busiest with soccer or when you may have more free time. They also may be able to suggest other sports that will actually help your soccer game.

Joy Fawcett

I once talked with Heather O'Reilly, who's on the national team, as she was preparing for the under-19 Women's World Cup. She said, "We are burnt out." And I'm thinking, "You are only 18 years old!" That's scary to me, and that's something that coaches should be aware of. In the development of the game these players shouldn't burn out at such a young age. If they do,

Shannon
MacMillan

Cindy Parlow has a street named after her in Memphis, Tennessee: "Cindy Parlow Drive."

they're not going to be around for the long haul when we need them.

 **Hope Solo**
I definitely have suffered through burnout. It has a lot to do with my time management skills, which aren't the best in the world. When I was traveling for a regional team, the whole time I was stressed because I had stuff that I needed to take care of at home. Every time I walked out on the field, my mind wouldn't be perfectly set in the right place.

Stressful moments will also burn you out. It is important to take a break from soccer, especially if you never take time off. I

Cindy Parlow

sometimes played for three teams in one season: the national team, an under-21 team, and college. It would get really, really hard. What helped me was having a few key people that I could just release everything to. There were nights where I went crying to my roommate. It doesn't necessarily help change things as far as you being pulled in every direction. But it's just nice to know that people understand and someone's there right along with you. I never would let anyone

Our Favorites

Hobbies

Kylie Bivens
Rollerblading

Kristen Luckenbill
Snowboarding

Kristine Lilly
Listening to music

Abby Wambach
Playstation® II

LaKeysia Beene
Bodyboarding

know I was stressed. I always wanted everyone to know that I could handle it and I was doing fine. But finally I just broke down and let it go. It was the best thing I could have done. I wish I had done it sooner.

Christie Welsh

I actually thought I was immune to burnout. Then after my freshman season at Penn State, I took the entire spring semester off to train and try to make the Olympic roster. I went all through my college season straight into residency with the women's national team and basically did everything with them up until August right before they went to the Olympics. I had to come back to Penn State that August and start preseason again. And at that point there was a good month where I was just struggling. It was like I didn't want to be there. I just felt tired all the time. How did I deal with it? I just took a little time off to relax and try to do other things. What I've learned from that experience is to keep a balance of doing different things including soccer. If you want soccer to be the number one thing that's fine, but somewhere in there do a balance of other things. For me that's playing racquetball and reading books. After a month or so off, I missed being back with my team. I wanted to be out there again playing with them. When I did, I was rejuvenated and excited again about soccer.

 ## Callie Withers

I've seen some people face burnout, and I think it has to do with overbearing parents. When the parents are into it more than their kids—that's bad. The kid feels the pressure to keep playing only for them. In my case, I put more pressure on myself because I knew I had potential. Other people saw that potential in me too, and it was just a vicious cycle of me working harder because I didn't want to let people down. When I finally took some time away from the game, I remembered why I really loved it. Soccer had always been fun. I learned then to not be so hard on myself, and I made sure that the game was fun for me.

 ## Cindy Parlow

Obviously soccer is a huge part of everyone's life when they reach the college and professional level. If it's your passion you still need to make sure it doesn't become your entire life. The most successful players manage their time. Family and friends remain very important. Maintaining those relationships and finding other things that you enjoy doing—hobbies, arts and crafts, shopping, or movies—it's just finding a balance, not having soccer be everything you are.

BEING YOUR BEST

By having a good circle of friends and family, you can become a better soccer player.

—Abby Wambach

 *What are the different ingredients that make up a top-level soccer player? There is a lot more to it than just what happens on the soccer field. Is our skill level important? Sure. Do we need to be competitive? You bet. These are obvious characteristics. But there are also many more pieces to becoming a successful soccer player.*

Jennifer Tietjen-Prozzo

To be a good soccer player I think you have to be well-rounded. You have to be a team player and have good communication and social skills. You have to be able to learn, to listen, take advice, and take criticism.

Shannon MacMillan

You have to have a passion for the game. You have to truly enjoy what you are doing out there. If you are not having fun, it's just not worth it. I'll hang up my cleats the day it's not fun. I also think you have to be willing to learn from everyone. From each player I can take a little something, and the same goes for each coach I have played under. The day I say I know it all, that's when I start the downhill slide.

Abby Wambach

By having a good circle of friends and family, you can become a better soccer player. I can't stress that enough. If it weren't for my parents and their love and willingness to take off every weekend to go to soccer tournaments with me, I would not have made it to the WUSA. So much has to come from your parents, whether it be money, attention, or support.

Danielle Slaton

Obviously all of the people at the professional level are very talented. They've done a lot to get to this point. I think the difference between the best professional player and the borderline professional player is very minimal. It's incredibly small. So one of the best traits a professional player can have is being willing to learn more and not being satisfied with, "Oh, I'm a professional athlete, and I'm pretty much the best at what I do." I'm in the top 2% of what I do, but I know that I can still get better.

When she's not playing soccer, Tiffeny Milbrett likes cooking and playing golf.

Briana Scurry

To be a good soccer player, athletic ability obviously helps. But soccer is a game where you can excel and not be the most athletic person. In soccer you can be short or tall, incredibly fit or not so fit, a fast runner or relatively slow. There is a position for every kind of player. What you should do is always try to improve. Remember that you'll have strengths when you play and you'll have weaknesses. Try to maximize the strengths, but don't forget about the weaknesses and try to gloss over them. You have to improve. You have to go out there and work on what you are not good at just as often as you work at what you are good at doing.

Kristine Lilly

A good soccer player has to work hard and be herself. You can't be someone else. So if you think someone else has a way of doing things that you think is great, you can take different pieces of that and incorporate it into how you practice and play, but you still need to be yourself. Learn from watching others but don't try to be them.

LaKeysia Beene

I think your desire and commitment to go out there every day makes for a good soccer player. Sometimes you might be afraid to put yourself on the line because you might

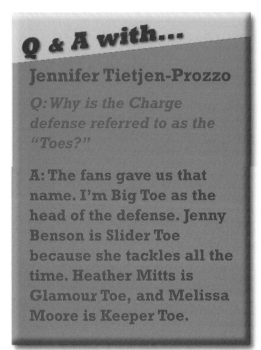

Q & A with...

Jennifer Tietjen-Prozzo

Q: Why is the Charge defense referred to as the "Toes?"

A: The fans gave us that name. I'm Big Toe as the head of the defense. Jenny Benson is Slider Toe because she tackles all the time. Heather Mitts is Glamour Toe, and Melissa Moore is Keeper Toe.

fail. That will only hold you back. All of us make mistakes. If you are committed to going out there to try your best, you will be surprised at what postitive things will happen.

It's important to work hard and be yourself, but you also need to work on technical skills and really understand how the game works. A lot of value is placed on athletic ability, and it is important. Ability must always be paired with a winning personality and strong people skills. Remember, soccer is a group sport, and while there are "stars" on every team, it takes the full effort of everyone to become a winning franchise.

Jennifer Grubb

To be a good soccer player I think you need tactical awareness. The physical tools help, but if you don't understand the game then you're lost. If you don't understand where the ball needs to go or the way in which you need to pass it, then you aren't going to succeed.

Carla Overbeck

One important aspect is being able to "read" the game. Also, because soccer is a team sport, you have to be a good teammate. Be a leader. Make sure that you're getting the best out of yourself and also your teammates.

Tiffany Roberts

A good soccer player is a leader who sets good examples for teammates. A leader is a person who inspires the rest of the team. I like setting a good example. I'm a captain on the Courage because I'm vocal. On the field I talk to my teammates, and I try to motivate them. I keep a positive attitude no matter what is going on. I also like to lead by example. So when I don't see my teammates hustling or going for the ball I say to myself, "I'm going to be the next one to go all out. I'm going for that ball so I hope I can inspire you."

 ## Melissa Moore

I think communication is probably one of the most important things necessary to become a good soccer player. Not only do you have to be physically fit but you also have to be knowledgeable about the game. You have to be able to read the game. For me, I probably lack a little bit in physical abilities, but I'm smart enough to read the game. You have to know what to say and when to work with your teammates—giving directions or providing encouragement. You don't exactly have to be the fastest person or the one who jumps the highest, but if you can read the game then you can put yourself in position to win the ball. If you are smart enough I think that you can make up for some physical shortcomings.

Most Embarrassing Moment

"Once I was defending in a game at Santa Clara. There was no one within 10 yards of me, but I tripped over my own feet and fell. The girl dribbling the ball blew right by me, and my friends and family still laugh about seeing my rear end sticking up in the air!"

-Danielle Slaton

Jenny Benson

There are days when you just don't feel like getting out there and playing, but it's your job, and when you get out there you've got to be prepared to give 100% for your teammates and yourself. So to be a good soccer player, you have to be ready to go every day. If you're mentally tough then you usually can get out there and push through almost anything.

Lorrie Fair

It's the stuff that you do when no one is watching that makes you a good soccer player. The training you do on your own. I never thought of it as training on my own. I always thought of it as, "I'm going out to play." Whether it was by myself, with my sister, or with my best friend, it wasn't like, "Oh, I have to do this because I have to be better than everybody else." I just wanted to. All the extra stuff that you do puts you so far ahead of everybody your age that you can start to play with people older than you. So you can either sit back and say, "Oh, I'm the youngest. So I don't have to be the best," or you can say, "I want to be the best," and move up that way. The difference between a professional and just a player is your ability to play and adapt to whatever team you are on. But at the same time, be an individual and be the player that can make the difference in the game.

Julie Foudy

The most important aspect of being a good player is to understand your role within a group because it's not an individual sport. You have to be willing to step out on the field whether it be practice or a game and show your team that you're going to work as hard as you can every time. That's critical.

Mia Hamm

TONY DiCICCO

Soccer is a team game with great individuals. In basketball, without a Diana Taurasi, UConn couldn't have won the 2003 Women's NCAA Basketball Championship. But she's got to fit into the team. The challenge of coaching is to create great individuals and then use that flair and that individual ability in a way that helps the whole team. Mia Hamm is a great individual player. She's also a great team player. One of my concerns is seeing a young Mia Hamm-type player in a youth game, dribbling through the other team while the parents and the coaches are yelling, "Pass the ball, pass the ball!" She's getting a mixed message. I don't think there were a lot of people on the sideline yelling to Allen Iverson to pass the ball. He learned to be able to beat people and go to the bucket. His coaches have used that talent so that he can go to the basket or dish it off to open players. That's an example of great individual skills fitting into a team concept. Coaches have to allow players to develop personalities on the field. In many cases we are inhibiting that.

Cindy Parlow

It's important to be a team player. I've never won a single game by myself. I can do what I do best and try to bring that to every game, but if you asked people on the national team if they were a ball hog, most of them would be like "Yeah, I get accused of that." In their case that is not really true. What those players all have in common is that they are hungry for the ball, especially when the game is on the line. Each knows that when the opportunity comes she can get it done, but she also knows that getting the ball to her teammates is just as valuable.

Kylie Bivens

Kristine Lilly

Abby Wambach

Being the youngest of seven children I've been a team player my whole life, so it hasn't been a big issue for me. I think the one thing you have to learn about being a team player is that whether you touch the ball or not you are still doing something. I think that's important for young girls to know.

 ### Kristin Luckenbill

I think it's hard to understand teamwork at a young age. You are trying to make an impression, but a lot of girls will dribble around thinking they're showing off their skills. That always made me mad. I could never make the team because I'd just be standing in the middle and no one would notice me. I was dishing the ball off to everyone else which was helping the team, but the kids who scored the goals got the attention. Everyone thinks the superstar dribbler is great. But oftentimes that person is hurting the team overall. It definitely takes all people on a team to make you win. Even the people on the bench. I don't mean just winning a game but having a winning season.

Our Favorites

Pigout Food

LaKeysia Beene – Cap'n Crunch® cereal

Julie Foudy – Brownies

Briana Scurry – Ice cream

Joy Fawcett – Reese's® Peanut Butter Cups

Carrie Moore

I'd say as a defender it's easier to be a team player. You definitely have to do that to be successful. To be a team player you have to pass it to someone who's wide open. Don't even think that you don't like her or you are mad at her that day. The only way you are going to have success as a team is if you play as a team.

Melissa Moore

I think there are certain people who have extra ability and they shine, but I think that in order to be successful you have to be a team player. One person is not going to win a game. It's the team. One person may stand out, but whether or not they get a goal or an assist depends on their teammates. Ask yourself, "Am I happy that I scored two goals even though we lost, or do I like the feeling of winning even though I never put the ball in the net?"

 ## Jennifer Tietjen-Prozzo

Being a team player means giving your all for the team. Going out and playing and scoring a goal or being a ball hog and just doing what you want for yourself hurts the team. To be a team player means doing what you have to do to help the team. Even if it means sitting on the bench for a game.

 ## Kristine Lilly

Teamwork means learning the game and learning when it's a good time to kick the ball and when it's a good time to pass. You need to know when it's your opportunity to take a shot or when there's an opportunity to pass it to someone else. You've just got to find a balance. There are times when you are the best player that day, and that's your time to take over and finish the game off. And then there are times when you aren't having a great day, and you should lay it across the goal mouth to someone else. It's all about how you work together as a team.

 ## LaKeysia Beene

You can't win the game alone. You have to have the defense to defend the goal and the offense to score. You can't go out and score by yourself. Sure certain players are in position to be the goal scorers and others just to defend, but many times it's what the defender did that starts the chain reaction that results in a goal. On the other hand, the best play a forward might make the entire game is a defensive one that stops the other team from getting something going.

Lorrie Fair

Jenny Benson

Everyone's got to work together. In Philadelphia, we really emphasize making each other better players and playing to each other's strengths. If I make the player next to me better, she's going to make me a better player, which will make our team a better team.

Lorrie Fair

There's no way you can win without your team- mates. The ball moves faster than any one player dribbling can carry it. It's like we can move the ball up the field as a unit and each person depends on the other person's pass, the other person's run, and the other person's body language. Do whatever it takes to succeed as a team.

Joy Fawcett

Teamwork is knowing that you're out there working hard and that your teammates are working just as hard as you. Everyone gets the praise when the team wins, and that's what team sports are all about. It takes everyone to win. You can't just have one person or even two or three to win. It takes everyone on the field and everyone to work hard. That's why any team that does well is one that is willing to work hard for each other and support and cover for each other.

Kylie Bivens

I think that teamwork really starts with being friends with your teammates—trusting them on and off the field. There are times when my teammates can't do something, but I'm going to do it because they are my friends and because I know they would do it for me. So it's kind of a balancing act. It makes you feel good too.

Danielle Slaton

I definitely think that part of the reason I love soccer is because I get to know 20 other players. I love the fact that 20 other players on the Carolina Courage have inspired me and help me when I'm struggling. I know that they can lean on me and I can lean on them when the times get tough. When times are great you have somebody to celebrate with. I definitely think that we couldn't have won the Founder's Cup if we weren't all solid together, willing to sacrifice for each other out there on the field. I think that's part of the reason we won. You have to do it as a team. That's going to make you win.

Tiffany Roberts

When I talk about teamwork, the main thing I talk about is having team chemistry. I look back at my teams that have won championships, and those teams are the ones that had great chemistry. We really respected each other. When you respect each other then that makes you want to play for one another, and you are proud of each other. If someone makes a mistake, you want to run over there and get the ball for them and make them look good by cleaning up. It's all about how well you work together.

Shannon MacMillan

I think teamwork is very important. If I wanted to play an individual sport I would have chosen tennis or track, but for me I like the fact that you have to be accountable to your teammates. Those days when it's raining and you don't want to go outside and work out, you think, "What's Joy Fawcett doing? I know she's out there." So that little drive and being able to rely on them when you are down helps tremendously. Then one day you are going to return the favor for them. It's a big sisterhood that we've created. It's really an extended family. We've shared the highs and lows of life from divorce to babies to victories to losses. It's the stuff that melds you together for life.

GAME DAY: GETTING READY

I don't do well when I go into games feeling tense and thinking too much about what I need to be doing.

—Julie Foudy

TONY DiCICCO

When we look at soccer athletes we measure them using four criteria: Tactical, the decision-making of the game; Technical, the skill part of the game—passing the ball from point A to point B, shooting it, heading it, whatever; Physical, which can be achieved on the field and in the weight room, adding both speed and power; then Psychological, such as dealing with adversity, maintaining the love for the game, keeping yourself enthusiastic, dealing with mistakes, and all the things that the top athletes face. Some athletes are able to play no matter if they are playing well or if they are playing poorly. Either way they are prepared to take the next shot, especially when the game is on the line.

What do we do to maximize our performance on the field? We recommend making sure two things are in good shape: Your body and your mind. It makes sense to have a plan for how you prepare for game day. However, all of us in the WUSA agree that the work you do weeks and months in advance is the vital ingredient to being prepared to play.

Danielle Slaton

To make sure I am at my best when I step on the field to play a game I have set goals—usually two or three that I want to work on for the game. For me it might be as simple as saying, "I want to be first to the ball," or "I want to make sure I am communicating to my teammates." That gets me focused and mentally prepared for the battle that I am going to have. It's not always just about skill and who's faster or who can kick the ball farthest. It's about who's going to bounce back when a goal gets scored against you or who's going to continue to work hard when things aren't going exactly as planned. I'm constantly thinking about what I can do better or what I can do to improve my game. That usually means going to talk to my coaches to ask for help. You've got to do that or else you are cheating yourself.

Melissa Moore

I'm most successful if I can visualize the game and do a mental run-through of how I want to perform. I think about what might happen in the game and in certain situations if I can come up with a save. Just before the game I like to relax. I don't even think about the game because I don't want to get too nervous. So I'll just goof off with my friends a little bit and maybe ten minutes before the game I'll settle down and relax and try to refocus. Otherwise I will get over-anxious.

Nel Fettig

On game day I try to keep my mind off the game until I'm on the field. I do a lot of crossword puzzles. I have the *New York Times* delivered to my house just for that reason. To prepare to play I make sure I eat right, rest, and do what I can to keep my mind focused on something else. It's important to stay relaxed and calm. For me that's crosswords, reading, anything like that.

Brandi Chastain

I'm a very intense person on the field, but I am also very jovial and lighthearted by nature. I've gone through many stages in my career where I allowed my emotions and my intensity to get the better of me and ruin what probably could have been really good situations. Those have been hard but valuable lessons. I try to go out and enjoy the game. You will see me smile and laugh a lot during games even though they are very hard. Say to yourself, "What happens when times are hard? What kind of person am I?" If you get upset, it's going to hurt you and your team. If you keep the mindset that this is a game and it's fun, you'll be much better off.

Julie Foudy

I don't do well when I go into games feeling tense and thinking too much about what I need to be doing. I can't have too many things on my brain. So just before a game I'm kind of hyper—just messing around, jumping around, not thinking about who we are about to play or what we have to do. Then when the game starts, I just go out with a positive attitude and give it my all.

 ### Shannon MacMillan

The night before, I start focusing on who we're playing, what I'm going to need to do. The next morning I get up with my dog, take him for a walk and have quiet time. A couple hours before the game I like to listen to music and just start chilling out. I start zoning in on what we have to do. I always make sure that I have thought about what I have to do so I am mentally ready for the game.

 ### Carla Overbeck

I've always taken a lot of pride in being one of the fittest people on the field. That takes a while to achieve. The older you get the more important it is that you have a plan to stay in shape. During the season it's easier. It's in the off-season that you better not turn into a couch potato. I certainly work on that, and I look at my game and see what I need to improve upon. I work on improving my weaknesses during the off-season. You can always improve on something. If you think you're done improving then you should probably stop playing because you can always get better.

Charmaine Hooper

It's so important to maintain your fitness. I may not be at my peak fitness all year round, but after the season I don't want to get too far out of shape. I try to maintain some sort of fitness so that when I have to get back into playing shape I don't have too far to go. As far as exercises or extra training outside of playing, I try to do strengthening exercises. I don't need to try to get stronger, but again I need to maintain strength and flexibility, which helps prevent injuries.

Briana Scurry

I do a lot of weight training. I started that in high school. When I step onto the field, I want to be the best that I can be. Whether that's going to be better than everybody else is not important to me. What's important is fulfilling my potential because I feel if I don't strive for that, I'm cheating myself.

Tiffany Roberts

It's up to you if you want to be committed to lifting weights, but I really like it. It makes me feel good. It definitely prepares me for playing. But it needs to be mixed with a lot of conditioning so I keep my cardiovascular system in top shape. What I do in the pre-season and in the off-season to maintain my fitness is such a key to being prepared to play. Once the season starts going, you're playing so much you don't want your body to break down by adding more on top of a full season of practice and games.

Tisha Venturini-Hoch

A big part for me to be prepared is based on what I do in the off-season. I spend a lot of time in the weight room. I do a lot of sprint type running and agility drills. I do some yoga to stretch out. I do some things that I don't get to do during the season like ride my mountain bike. I also watch tapes of games and become a student of the game. I can pick up ideas on how I can be a better player and see things I need to do to improve my skills.

Most Embarrassing Moment

"I tripped on the metal rim of a track next to the field I was playing on. I fell on my face in front of all the fans!"
—Jennifer Tietjen-Prozzo

 *Another vital ingredient* in preparing for game day is deciding what you will eat. *We've all heard about nutrition, balanced diets, and the like. (We all like to pig out once in a while, too!) I can tell you from experience that what you eat is important, especially on game day.*

Briana Scurry

Three-and-a-half to four hours before a game I usually eat chicken and pasta. That's worked well for me because when I warm up I don't want to have my stomach gurgling because I ate too close to kickoff. I want to be able to have something for my body to use—to burn during the game. When I want to pigout, I like the sweet stuff. I really like ice cream. That's one of my weaknesses.

Mia Hamm

Before a game I eat a peanut butter and jelly sandwich. When I want to pigout, I go for chips and salsa.

Nel Fettig

My ideal pre-game meal would be a peanut butter and banana with honey sandwich. It sits so easily in my stomach. It sustains me for the four hours. Sometimes I will add some pretzels for more balance with a cup of water. My weakness is pizza. I love pizza. And any kind of ice cream. There are so many pigout foods. I love them all!

Leslie Gaston

I'm really not that picky. I make sure I drink a lot of water and I'm really well hydrated. I like baked potatoes or anything with a lot of carbohydrates. For pigging out I like Butterfingers®. I like to eat the chocolate off the outside first and then eat the underneath part. Those are my favorite. During the season when I was in school, I would have a Butterfinger every day.

Joy Fawcett

I have to have that peanut butter and jelly sandwich. When I get the urge, I have a Reese's® Peanut Butter Cup.

Tiffany Roberts

I have a new pre-game ritual—eating a banana, peanut butter, and honey sandwich. I like to eat healthy things. So I try to choose going the healthy route, but I'm not a health freak. I will put sour cream in my burrito or on my baked potato. The way that I look at it is to eat everything in the right proportions. For dessert I love ice cream, especially coffee ice cream.

Brandi Chastain

I'd say there are two different scenarios for game day meals. One is if you are on the road, and one is if you are at home. On the road it's a bit harder because you don't have your own stuff from your own kitchen. Other than that, the meals should be high in carbohydrates with some proteins thrown in there. And a lot of water. I'll eat about four hours beforehand and then maybe have a PowerBar® an hour before I go out to the field. When I'm being bad, I'll have vanilla swiss almond ice cream.

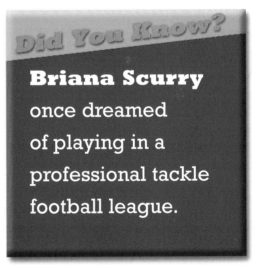

Did You Know?

Briana Scurry once dreamed of playing in a professional tackle football league.

Deliah Arrington

I like to have fruit, a turkey sandwich, and a granola bar right before a game—a little energy boost before I play. For my sweet tooth I go for Milk Duds®.

Mary McVeigh

I eat tons of pasta with meat sauce. My mom always told me to eat bananas. So I would always put them in a milkshake because I never liked them plain. Once I got to high school, I became a big fan of steak. My mom would always make me steak the night before a big game.

Cindy Parlow

I usually eat a meal high in carbohydrates with some protein—something pretty low in fat. I'll have some pasta with some marinara sauce or maybe a turkey sandwich. If I want to pigout, it's just about anything my mom cooks. She's an amazing cook, and I get so excited when I go home to visit because I know the whole time I'm there I'm going to have great meals.

Carla Overbeck

I pretty much eat whatever I want to eat. I don't have a set thing. I'll eat burgers and steaks and chicken. My favorites are Mexican food and chocolate. Not a lot of stuff with nuts but things like Hershey® bars or CRUNCH® bars. I really love chocolate!

Kristine Lilly

As professional players, we get a lot of nutritional talks. We're told to eat a balanced diet and not to exclude anything from our diet. If anything, we don't eat enough calories. Females tend to eat fewer calories than needed, so we're pretty much encouraged to eat more throughout the day. When I'm not thinking about whether something is good for me, I love chocolate chip cookie dough ice cream.

Shannon MacMillan

I think nutrition is something that can give you an extra edge. When you need a little bit of edge to beat your opponent, something like nutrition can come into play. Late in the game when they are tiring if you are taking care of your body and eating healthy you can get that extra little surge. That might be that step you need to get that shot off or to poke the ball away as they are running at you. With all that said, I love doughnuts. I have a weakness for chocolate doughnuts.

Abby Wambach

I eat four or five times a day. The more often you eat, the faster your metabolism and the more you'll burn off during the day. My favorite pigout meal is a hot dog with cheese, chili, and ketchup.

Charmaine Hooper

What may work for somebody else may not work for you. I try to see how certain types of proteins work for me. I try to consume a few more carbohydrates a couple of days before games just to give me a little extra energy. I love cake and ice cream.

Mia Hamm

Julie Foudy

Marinette Pichon

I eat pasta, chicken, and I like steak. That's very good. Before I lived in the U.S., I never had ice cream, and now I love it. My favorite flavor is peanut butter and coconut.

Melissa Moore

My pre-game meal is pancakes and bacon. I just try to eat healthy. I try not to go eat hamburgers every-day. Maybe once a week. I like pizza for sure. I believe everybody likes pizza!

Julie Foudy

As I've gotten older, I've been much better about trying to eat better by being conscious about balance. I could live on carbs, but I need the protein and the iron. I make a con-scious effort to eat vegetables, meat, and fish. I stay away from fried foods. I'm a huge fan of dessert—anything fattening like brownies or ice cream!

DARING
TO DREAM

*Set goals and set them high, but
be ready so that when the
roadblocks come you'll know
how to handle them.*

—Shannon MacMillan

TONY DiCICCO

You've got to have a dream, whether it's to be President of the United States or to be an Olympic athlete. It's got to be a vivid dream. It can't be, "I just want to make the team" or " I just want to go as far as I can in the sport." Then you've got to write down your plan for achieving that dream because it's not going to happen by itself. Your action plan may be to train two times a week with your team but to work more on specific skills in your backyard. The great players achieve ultimate success because they are doing that little bit of extra work.

Here's the best part. You may never reach the dream you have in mind, but it's still good for you to go for it. You may work for three or four years to become an Olympic athlete but find when you are in college that you want to be a doctor. Even if you don't become an Olympic athlete you will still be in good physical shape, and you will have learned how to focus on a goal and be disciplined.

Young players and future players are always asking us for advice. We all remember the best advice we ever got, because good advice stays with you for a long time. Most of us have heard that you can't get anywhere in soccer or in life if you don't work hard and have a deep commitment to what you are doing. That's really true. Sometimes we try too hard in life to control the things that happen to us, but often the best advice is to do your best and just see what happens. We think it's very important to find what it is you love to do and have fun doing it.

Deliah Arrington

Don't take this game too seriously. It's not the most important thing in the world. I used to think it was when I was younger. When I had a bad game I was in shambles all week and I forgot this is supposed to be fun.

Briana Scurry

The best advice I ever got was always keep working and never stop having fun. It's amazing how far you can go if you just keep working at it. Just believe in yourself and surround yourself with people who believe in you as well.

 ## Nel Fettig

Always stay focused on what it is you want to do. I think if you are really determined to do something you can find a way to do it. No one should deter you from your goals, and you should always go after them. Some people do not look at their progression along the way. They only focus on the end result and don't realize that meanwhile they are becoming a better player.

 ## Kristine Lilly

Let bad things go no matter what you do. If you're playing and you're in a bad mood, that mood is not going to help you.

 ## Charmaine Hooper

Probably some of the best advice I've gotten from a coach is not to worry about things that are out of your control. The best thing you can do is just go out there and let your feet do the talking.

 ## Jennifer Tietjen-Prozzo

My first piece of advice would be never to be afraid to try something. The second would be never to be afraid to make a mistake. When trying something new, mistakes will be made, but you will also learn something.

 ## Brandi Chastain

My grandfather taught me a lesson when I was young. He came to all of my games, and he used to give me a dollar if I scored a goal, but if I got an assist he'd give me a dollar-fifty. So he instilled in me the idea that it was better to give than to receive, and the idea of sharing became very important.

Shannon MacMillan

I think you've just got to find what's right for you. You're the one who's got to do it. Don't do things just because your friends are doing them—that only lasts for so long. Whether it's soccer, another sport, academics, or music, you've just got to try everything and see what works for you and what makes you truly happy as a person.

Tiffany Roberts

I train kids and I always say, "You want to be out here, right?" Because if you don't *want* to be out training then you're not going to get anything out of it. So I'm always telling kids, as long as you're having fun and you have a lot of passion for what you do then you are going to excel no matter what it is. That's what happened to me when I fell in love with soccer. All I wanted to do was to be the best because I loved it so much.

Hope Solo

Play what you want to play. Play volleyball *and* soccer. A lot of people tried to force me to decide between the two at a younger age than I really had to. I see a lot of young girls being cornered into making a choice, and by the time they are seniors in high school, they're tired of that one sport. I think other sports help balance things out. It helps your athleticism, but also it teaches you to be well-rounded.

Did You Know?

Christie Pearce is a talented seamstress and avid sewer. In high school she made her own prom dress!

 *When it comes to improving your soccer skills, our advice is to get the basic technical skills down and compete with people who will make you better.*

Lorrie Fair

 Don't be afraid to compete. You may not want to upset your friends, but I was lucky enough that I found friends that could just totally go at it. We were always competing, but at the same time that's what brought the best out in each of us.

Briana Scurry

 I tell young girls to try to play with players who are better than they are so that they can improve. I always suggest to parents that if you see some talent there, try to get your child with people older so the game is faster and they have to adapt and adjust and think more quickly. Don't keep them in an area where they dominate the game year after year and don't improve.

Tisha Venturini-Hoch

 Get the basics down. Learn how to get the ball and control it. You need to learn how to pass the ball correctly with the right pace. Learn to feel comfortable with the ball as early as possible. From the age of six to ten years old, I was always messing around with the ball somehow.

Jennifer Tietjen-Prozzo

 When I go out and do clinics, I tell young girls they have to learn to play every position on the field, including goalkeeper. That's going to make you learn the game much better. Then you can find a position that you really feel comfortable with or that you like the best.

Abby Wambach

 The one piece of advice I would give is to find a role model. It's great to have somebody to look to, to guide where you need to go, but don't try to be exacty like them. You can't mimic somebody else. Mia Hamm has been a huge star and huge idol for me, and now I am on the flip side where I'm friends with her. Even though I've looked at her my whole career and said, "Wow, I want to get where she is," I never said I want to be *just like* Mia.

Danielle Slaton

I tell young girls that they need to want to be a professional soccer player, but they also need to want to be themselves when they grow up. For example, I don't want you to be just like me—I want you to be the best person you can be, but also make sure you take time away from soccer. I take a month off, and then I'm really excited and I can't wait to get back on the field.

To reach the highest level in any sport, it's important to set goals along the way. Not only should you set long-term goals but also short-term goals. You may find that the goals you set need to be adjusted when you hit roadblocks or obstacles.

Q & A with...

Abby Wombach

Q: *How important is education to athletes these days?*

A: It is absolutely ESSENTIAL to have a college degree! If I weren't in the WUSA right now I would be in school getting my degree.

There are many ways to position yourself to play soccer professionally. Most will agree that you have to play as much as you can, but remember to enjoy the journey on the way to your goal. Don't wait until you reach your goal to have fun and be happy, or you'll miss too many good things!

Tiffany Roberts

In second grade, my teacher asked us to draw a picture of what our goals were in life. I drew a picture of me on top of an Olympic podium with all these gold medals around my neck. I have that evidence to show that I really had dreams when I was young. It's important to set goals, and things can really happen like that if you put your mind to it.

Julie Foudy

You have to have different types of goals. You need to have long-term goals, which are in the distant future, and then you have to have goals that you can achieve in the short term. I think they're critical because you need some gauge of where you're going and where you've been. I've gotten much better at setting goals over the years. I wish I had been better at it at a younger age.

Lorrie Fair

The key is to take one step at a time. I said to myself, "Well, I just want to make this district team. I want to make state tryouts. I want to do well at regionals. I want to be invited to the regional camp. I want to make the regional team. I want to travel with them and score a goal or two." Then all of a sudden things started falling into place. The next thing I knew I got a phone call saying, "We want you to come in for this under-16 national camp. Then I got called up for the national team the next year. So things can move quickly if you set short, small goals.

MY MOTTO

"Be disciplined and work hard... but have fun!"

-Nel Fettig

Shannon MacMillan

In high school, I didn't really know about the national team or anything like that. I only knew soccer was going to be a tool to get me into college. I knew I was going to put everything into it because I wanted to go to school. So you've got to set goals along the way, but you have to be willing to readjust them as you go. If soccer hadn't gotten me into college, of course it would have been devastating, but I would have had to reevaluate and find another way. Set goals and set them high, but be ready so that when the roadblocks come you'll know how to handle them.

> **Did You Know?**
>
> **Kate Sobrero** once had to dye her hair red because she lost a bet. She played the rest of the World Cup Quarterfinals as a redhead!

Carrie Moore

My advice to parents is to give kids every opportunity to play. Encourage them if they want to play, but definitely don't push them or force things. The more kids play, the better they will get.

Abby Wambach

Nowadays they have younger girls playing soccer all year round. When I was younger, I needed a winter off to play basketball, to get my mind off of soccer. I didn't want to give up my free time because I knew later on in my career I wouldn't be able to do that. I think it's important to live your life doing some things that you like. It can't be all work or all soccer.

Melissa Moore

It's difficult because at ten, I would say just go out and have fun. I didn't even get serious about soccer until high school. If you enjoy soccer and you like to go out and practice every day then do that. However, if you are tired and don't want to practice then take a day off. If you are ten years old, you are supposed to enjoy what you are doing. You're not supposed to be dwelling on how you are going to get a scholarship for college!

 *How much commitment does it take to reach the level of playing in the WUSA? Young girls have to do many things to make it far in soccer. It's not just luck or being in the right place at the right time that gets us here. It takes focus, determination, and sacrifice.*

 ## Nel Fettig

It's not going to happen overnight. You can't build a huge wall without putting each brick in. So what it takes is a focus on individual things. Focus on each step of what it takes to get to the desired result. Whether it's working on your speed, your fitness, your ball skills—each year you can focus on one thing. If you don't focus, you can lose sight of what it takes to achieve that goal.

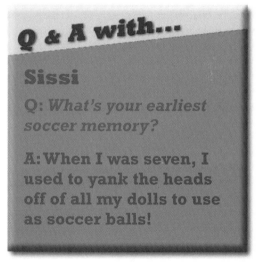

Q & A with...

Sissi

Q: *What's your earliest soccer memory?*

A: When I was seven, I used to yank the heads off of all my dolls to use as soccer balls!

Shannon MacMillan

To reach the WUSA level takes a lot of sacrifice. In high school I think I went to one prom—one homecoming. In college I spent my spring breaks training while other students were going off having the vacation of a lifetime. But when I finally got to the WUSA, I realized I would do it again in a heartbeat.

Danielle Slaton

To reach this level, you need to be in an environment where you have an opportunity to train and to play against players who are better than you so you can continue to improve. But that's not going to be the case for everybody. Maybe you don't have all the resources that other players or schools may have, but you are willing to go out and say, "Look, this is what I have, and this is what I want to do." Find the people who can help you. Whether that means going to find somebody to coach you or calling colleges and saying, "Look, I want to play soccer in college. How can I do that at your school? Can we work to find something to make this possible for me?" Do whatever it takes.

Charmaine Hooper

The best thing you can do is to set your goals and go out to achieve them. I don't think you should let anyone tell you that something is not obtainable—that you can't accomplish a certain goal because you are too short, too tall, not skinny enough, or whatever. You have a special quality. You may not be the fastest player or have the best technique, but there's some quality within you that makes you a great player.

Tiffany Roberts

I think everyone just needs to find that one really special quality. Everyone's quality is different. But as a pro you can't just have that quality and then nothing else. You need to be good at everything and then also have this one outstanding quality that puts you over the top. I think the quality that puts me over the top is my defensive presence and my aggressiveness. So if you want to be a professional soccer player, find out what you are good at doing.

FINDING SUCCESS

*Luckily, I was encouraged to
be competitive because my
family is pretty competitive. I
would do whatever it took to be
better and to win.*

—Nel Fettig

 *To help you reach success, we identified things that above all else were instrumental in getting us to the top of our game. There are many experiences and characteristics that we think have been key to our success. Sometimes success can change you, so we've included some thoughts about that, too.*

 ### Kylie Bivens

The feedback that I got from coaches helped me a lot. I was always told I could do better if I worked on this or that and that there was no one who could really hold me back. The coaches that I came in contact with when I was in seventh or eighth grade told me that if I kept working on various skills and techniques there would be no limit to where I could go.

 ### Lorrie Fair

As a kid I was faster than everybody. I was also aggressive and more competitive. I was just born that way. My sister and my brother were like that too, and my brother would take every opportunity to challenge me to some sort of game—like a staring contest or laughing contest. Everything was a competition, even seeing who could get to the bathroom first! What I did as a kid made competing on the soccer field seem normal.

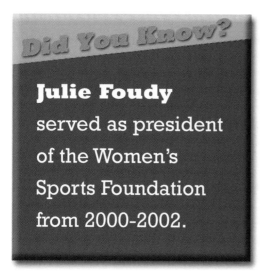

Did You Know?

Julie Foudy served as president of the Women's Sports Foundation from 2000-2002.

 ### Nel Fettig

My endurance and my perseverance helped me go far in soccer. At an early age there are kids who are more coordinated than others, but it takes more than just natural ability. Luckily, I was encouraged to be competitive because my family is pretty competitive. The school I went to had a lot of people who were driven. I truly enjoyed playing, but I also loved the opportunity to get out there and compete. That's what set me apart. I would do whatever it took to be better and to win.

Tisha Venturini-Hoch

Balancing things in your life is important. I love the sport, but I also did a lot of other things. I was involved in the student body, and I played in the band when I was younger. I had a lot of friends outside of soccer. Playing other sports helped me not to take soccer for granted. A lot of kids nowadays are just doing soccer—that's it. They do extra clinics in camp, and I'm afraid many of these kids are going to be worn out or they're going to turn away from the sport.

Q & A with...

Katia

Q: *What's your earliest soccer memory?*

A: Trespassing on a private field to play soccer, then running away when the owner came!

Kristine Lilly

Playing with the boys was a big factor in my success. They were stronger and sometimes faster. Definitely rougher. I had to keep up, and that prepared me for what was to come later in soccer.

Shannon MacMillan

My decision to go to the University of Portland and play for Clive Charles has a lot to do with my success. When I left high school, I was a very shy and timid person and really had no sense of my own value.

I went on my recruiting trip with Clive. I wasn't highly recruited by other schools, and Portland called out of the blue. The whole weekend, Clive didn't say a word to me. Then he brought

Our Favorites

Pigout Food

Mia Hamm – Chips and salsa

Kristine Lilly – Chocolate chip cookie dough ice cream

Shannon MacMillan – Doughnuts

Abby Wambach – Hot dog with cheese, chili, and ketchup

me in his office right before the end of the visit. He said, "I've watched you with the girls. We think you are going to fit in. We want to offer you a scholarship." I said, "Okay, but what about playing time?" He said "What about it?" I said, "Well other coaches have told me I'm going to be a starter. I'm going to score this many goals." He looked at me and said, "I can't tell you that. Whether you start or not and how well you do depends on what you do when you get here and how happy you are as a person." I just remember being blown away by that. From that day on, anytime he spoke or coached I was just a sponge, absorbing everything he threw at me. He really helped me develop.

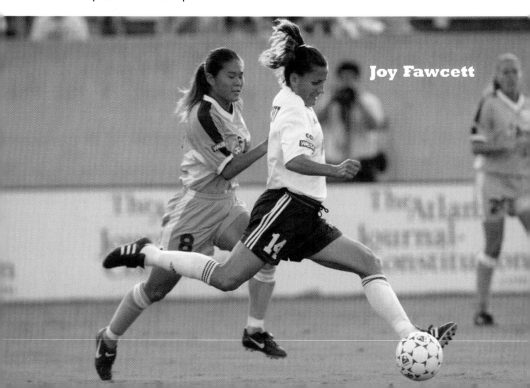

Joy Fawcett

Carla Overbeck

My family has played such a big role in my soccer career. They're very strong, and my parents and brothers and sister are extremely supportive—not just in my soccer career, but in everything I do. I'm just fortunate to have a great family to look up to and help me make good decisions.

Briana Scurry

My parents' positive support was the biggest part of my success, and it still is. I cannot recall a single time that my parents ever said no to anything involving soccer or any other sport, with maybe one exception. (They thought ice hockey was kind of dangerous.)

Sports involve a major time commitment. They took me to every tournament and every practice—and I played sports year round. They were constantly driving me all over the place. My parents did it all and never complained. That left a very positive feeling in my life. They also allowed me to make decisions. I wasn't always right, but it helped me learn that what became of me was really up to me. When it was time to choose a college, they left the final decision to me: "If you decide to go to UMass and you don't like it, that's the decision you made. We don't want to tell you to go someplace and then have you resent us if you don't like it." That helped me grow up as well.

Did You Know?

Breanna Boyd shares a birthday with Courage teammate Danielle Slaton: June 10, 1981.

Abby Wambach

There are so many things, so many coaches, and so many thoughts that have been a factor in my career. But I think the most important factor is to have support from your family.

Cindy Parlow

I'm a lot more outgoing than I used to be. Growing up, I was a pretty shy kid. I think as I've grown up and been a little bit in the spotlight, I've come out of my shell a lot more. It's given me a lot of confidence.

Carla Overbeck

I've always been very competitive, but at the same time you want people to like you and you want to have friends. I went to college this shy little freshman who cried every day and wanted to go home. By my senior year I was really enjoying school and just getting the most out of being a student athlete. The way that I matured in college was so great for me personally. It showed me that it's okay to be competitive at this level and even the next level. And you'll still have friends even if you beat them one day and they come back and beat you the next day.

Did You Know?

Brandi Chastain likes to garden. She has a great garden at home, and tending to her roses relaxes her when she's away from soccer.

Shannon MacMillan

When I first got to college, I would cry every day. I had no confidence and no sense of who I was as a person. As I grew older I became more confident on and off the field. It just happened. After college I learned that you could touch other people's lives. When someone comes up to you with your jersey on and says, "Can I have your autograph," it's the most powerful thing. "Wow," they'll tell you, "I saw you do this move, and I went home and tried it and watch—I can do this." That blows me away because when I was younger, I never had someone in the sport to watch and learn from.

Tiffeny Milbrett

Tiffany Roberts

I have gone from being an individual player to a team player. When I was 10 I liked scoring goals because I was a forward and I was fast. So to me having a successful game would be scoring all those goals for my team. Now I don't even think about scoring a goal. That's not even an objective of mine. If I get a goal I still get excited, but now I think my role is different. I like to win the balls for my team and give them up to other people to do what I used to like to do. For me to have a successful game I have to make a lot of good passes—giving the ball up so my team-mates can score.

MEET THE STARS OF THE WUSA

DELIAH ARRINGTON #10

THE BASICS:
Team: Philadelphia Charge
Position: Forward
College: Clemson
Hometown: Pawleys Island, SC
Born: May 5, 1981
Pawleys Island, SC
Height: 5' 5"

IMPRESSIVE FACTS:
While at Clemson, majored in biological sciences...named 2002 Atlantic Coast Conference Player of the Year (first Clemson women's player to receive this award).
*Deliah's favorite movie is *What's Eating Gilbert Grape*. Her motto is, "Live life to the fullest."

LaKEYSIA BEENE #1

THE BASICS:
Team: San Jose CyberRays
Position: Goalkeeper
College: Notre Dame
Hometown: Gold River, CA
Born: March 9, 1978
Shaw AFB, SC
Height: 5' 7"

IMPRESSIVE FACTS:
Majored in environmental geoscience at Notre Dame...named 2001 WUSA Goalkeeper of the Year...started playing soccer because all her friends played...has black belt in Karate.
*If her life were a song, it would be, "Shut Up and Dance!"

JENNY BENSON #6

THE BASICS:

Team: Philadelphia Charge
Position: Defender
College: University of Nebraska
Hometown: Huntington Beach, CA
Born: January 25, 1978
Fountain Valley, CA
Height: 5'5"

IMPRESSIVE FACTS:

Graduated from Nebraska in December 2000 with a degree in communication studies...honored with the 2002 Extra Effort Award by David Akers' Kicks for Kids.
*Jenny's favorite book is *The Pilot's Wife* by Anita Shreve.

KYLIE BIVENS #4

THE BASICS:

Team: Atlanta Beat
Position: Defender
College: Santa Clara University
Hometown: Upland, CA
Born: October 24, 1978 Claremont, CA
Height: 5' 5"

IMPRESSIVE FACTS:

Member of the inaugural WUSA All-Star South squad in 2002...1999 All-WCC and All-West Region player...named 1999 Santa Clara University defensive MVP.
*Kylie's favorite TV shows are "Road Rules" and "Real World."

BREANNA BOYD #8

THE BASICS:
Team: Carolina Courage
Position: Defender
College: University of Nebraska
Hometown: Calgary, AB, Canada
Born: June 10, 1981
Edmonton, Alberta, Canada
Height: 5' 8"

IMPRESSIVE FACTS:
Started 41 international matches for the Canadian National Team...member of 2002 First team for All-Big 12 conference. *One of Breanna's favorite foods is fudge. Her motto is, "Live every day like it's the last day."

THORI BRYAN #2

THE BASICS:
Team: San Jose CyberRays
Position: Defender
College: North Carolina State
Hometown: Wake Forest, NC
Born: April 27, 1974 Baltimore, MD
Height: 5' 8"

IMPRESSIVE FACTS:
Graduated from N.C. State with a bachelor of arts in sports management...in 2002, was the only CyberRays player - and one of only four league-wide - to play every minute of every regular-season match, a total of 21 games and 1,890 minutes. *The biggest obstacle of Thori's life so far has been dealing with her father's death.

BRANDI CHASTAIN #6

THE BASICS:

Team: San Jose CyberRays
Position: Defender
College: Santa Clara University
Hometown: San Jose, CA
Born: July 21, 1968 San Jose, CA
Height: 5'7"

IMPRESSIVE FACTS:

Graduated from Santa Clara with a degree in television communication...best known for scoring the game-winning goal in the 1999 World Cup championship match against China... member of the 1996 Olympic gold medal team.

LIFE BEYOND THE WUSA:

Gives speeches at high schools and businesses.
*Brandi's favorite TV show is anything on ESPN.

MARIBEL DOMINGUEZ #13

THE BASICS:

Team: Atlanta Beat
Position: Forward
Hometown: Mexico City, Mexico
Born: November 18, 1978
        Mexico City, Mexico
Height: 5' 4"

IMPRESSIVE FACTS:

Is the Mexican Women's National Team captain...recieved an honorable mention to the all-tournament team at the 2002 Gold Cup.
*Maribel's favorite actor is Brad Pitt. Her favorite singer is Shakira.

LORRIE FAIR #2

THE BASICS:

Team: Philadelphia Charge
Position: Midfielder
College: North Carolina
Hometown: Los Altos, CA
Born: August 5, 1978 Los Altos, CA
Height: 5' 3"

IMPRESSIVE FACTS:

Has an identical twin sister, Ronnie, who also plays in the WUSA with the San Diego Spirit...On May 9, 1997, the U.S. National Team played England, marking the first time sisters had played together for the U.S. National Team.
*Lorrie's pre-game ritual is to put on her left side clothing before her right.

JOY FAWCETT #14

THE BASICS:

Team: San Diego Spirit
Position: Defender
College: University of California
Hometown: Huntington Beach, CA
Born: February 8, 1968
         Inglewood, CA
Height: 5' 5"

IMPRESSIVE FACTS:
Named UCLA's first women's soccer coach May 25, 1993.

LIFE BEYOND THE WUSA:
Became the ultimate "Soccer Mom" during 1997 by simultaneously coaching at UCLA, coaching a youth club team, and playing for the national team while raising two children. A 3rd daughter was born in 2001.
*Joy's favorite movie is *Pretty Woman*.

NEL FETTIG #13

THE BASICS:
Team: Carolina Courage
Position: Defender
College: University of North Carolina
at Chapel Hill
Hometown: Fort Wayne, IN
Born: April 25, 1976 Fort Wayne, IN
Height: 5′ 4″

IMPRESSIVE FACTS:
Majored in psychology and exercise science at UNC...attended UNC Law School...placed on the Dean's List at UNC and ACC All-Academic Honor Roll...was her high school's class valedictorian.
*Nel's favorite food is shrimp and grits.

JULIE FOUDY #11

THE BASICS:
Team: San Diego Spirit
Position: Midfielder
College: Stanford University
Hometown: Mission Viejo, CA
Born: January 23, 1971 San Diego, CA
Height: 5′ 6″

IMPRESSIVE FACTS:
Earned her bachelor of science degree in biology from Stanford in 1993...broke new ground with her work as an in-studio analyst for ESPN's coverage of the 1998 World Cup...made a well-publicized trip to Pakistan in March of 1997 to observe the business of making soccer balls and make sure child labor was not involved...won the 1997 FIFA Fair Play Award for her work against child labor, the first woman and first American to win the award.

LESLIE GASTON #29

THE BASICS:

Team: Atlanta Beat
Position: Defender
College: University of North Carolina at Chapel Hill
Hometown: Montgomery, AL
Born: August 9, 1980 Montgomery, AL
Height: 5' 5"

IMPRESSIVE FACTS:

Named to the NSCAA All-American third team her senior year...named to the 2002 All-Southeast Region first team.
*Leslie's favorite food is vanilla ice cream with chocolate syrup. Her motto is, "Anything is possible."

JENNIFER GRUBB #14

THE BASICS:

Team: Washington Freedom
Position: Defender
College: Notre Dame
Hometown: Hoffman Estates, IL
Born: July 20, 1978 Elkhart, IN
Height: 5' 7"

IMPRESSIVE FACTS:

A three-time *Parade Magazine* and NSCAA High School All-American...lettered twice in football as a placekicker...was the first girl to score a point in Illinois high school football history.
*Jennifer's favorite hobbies are reading, writing, and being outdoors. Her motto is, "Do what makes you happy."

MIA HAMM #9

THE BASICS

Team: Washington Freedom
Position: Forward/Midfielder
College: University of North Carolina at Chapel Hill
Hometown: Austin, TX
Born: March 17, 1972 Selma, AL
Height: 5' 5"

IMPRESSIVE FACTS:

Won the 1998 ESPY Award for Outstanding Female Athlete at the ESPN annual awards show...the largest building at NIKE headquarters was named for her in 1999...among *People* magazine's 50 Most Beautiful People in 1997.

LIFE BEYOND THE WUSA:

Started the Mia Hamm Foundation in 1999 to benefit Bone Marrow Research.

DEVVYN HAWKINS #3

THE BASICS:

Team: Boston Breakers
Position: Midfielder
College: Santa Clara University
Hometown: Olympia, WA
Born: November 29, 1980 Sitka, AK
Height: 5' 8"

IMPRESSIVE FACTS:

Selected in the first round (3rd overall) in the 2003 WUSA draft...scored the "Golden Goal" in a 1-0 win over Germany to help the U.S. capture the Four Nations Tournament title in China on January 29, 2003...was part of Santa Clara's 2001 NCAA Championship Team that included Aly Wagner and Daniel Slayton.

CHARMAINE HOOPER #10

THE BASICS:

Team: Atlanta Beat
Position: Forward
College: North Carolina State
Hometown: Ottawa, ON, Canada
Born: January 15, 1968
Georgetown, Guyana
Height: 5'7"

IMPRESSIVE FACTS:

In 2002 was elected into the inaugural class of the United Soccer League's Hall of Fame...twice named a NSCAA All-American while at North Carolina State.
*Charmaine likes to wear stud earrings and gold nail polish. Her favorite skin care product is cocoa butter.

ANGELA HUCLES #11

THE BASICS:

Team: Boston Breakers
Position: Forward
College: University of Virginia
Hometown: Virginia Beach, VA
Born: April 5, 1978 Virginia Beach, VA
Height: 5' 7"

IMPRESSIVE FACTS:

Graduated in May 2000 with a degree in anthropology...member of the U.S. Under-20 National Team from 1997-1999...scored the first goal in Breakers history during preseason in a 3-0 victory over Duke in Durham, North Carolina on March 6, 2001.
*In her spare time Angela enjoys playing golf and watching basketball.

KATIA #9

THE BASICS:

Full Name: Katia Cilene Teixeira da Silva
Team: San Jose CyberRays
Position: Forward
Hometown: Sao Paulo, Brazil
Born: February 18, 1977
Rio de Janeiro, Brazil
Height: 5' 10"

IMPRESSIVE FACTS:

A heptathlete who finished fifth in the South American championships and broke the Brazilian national record six times.
*Katia enjoys listening to Madonna and JaRule.

LIFE BEYOND THE WUSA:

Katia likes to get involved with Christmas programs that help the needy.

JENA KLUEGEL #5

THE BASICS:

Team: Boston Breakers
Position: Defender
College: University of North Carolina
at Chapel Hill
Hometown: Mahtomedi, MN
Born: November 2, 1979 St. Paul, MN
Height: 5' 3"

IMPRESSIVE FACTS:

Selected in the 1st round (3rd overall) in the 2002 WUSA draft...named 2002 Breakers Rookie of the Year.
*Jena's favorite movie is *American Beauty*. She loves to eat burritos.

KRISTINE LILLY #13

THE BASICS:

Team: Boston Breakers
Position: Midfielder
College: University of North Carolina
Hometown: Wilton, CT
Born: July 22, 1971 New York, NY
Height: 5' 4"

IMPRESSIVE FACTS:

Graduated from The University of North Carolina with a degree in communications...a road sign entering her hometown reads, "Welcome to Wilton: Hometown of Olympic gold medallist Kristine Lilly"...the soccer field at her former high school in Wilton is named after her.

LIFE BEYOND THE WUSA:

Runs the Kristine Lilly Soccer Academy every summer in Wilton.

KRISTIN LUCKENBILL #2

THE BASICS:

Team: Carolina Courage
Position: Goalkeeper
College: Dartmouth
Hometown: Paoli, PA
Born: May 28, 1979 Paoli, PA
Height: 5' 9"

IMPRESSIVE FACTS:

Three-time All American and four-time All-Ivy selection at Dartmouth...1997 Ivy League Rookie of the Year...named 2002 WUSA Goalkeeper of the Year when she led the league in saves.
*Kristen's favorite food is sushi.

SHANNON MACMILLAN   #8

THE BASICS:

Team: San Diego Spirit
Position: Forward
College: University of Portland
Hometown: Escondido, CA
Born: October 7, 1974 Syosset, NY
Height: 5' 5"

IMPRESSIVE FACTS:

Majored in social work at Portland...appeared on the cover of *Sports Illustrated*'s daily Olympic issue after her goal against Norway in 1996...received the key to the city of Escondido in December of 1996 after winning her Olympic gold medal...was an assistant women's soccer coach at Portland and helped the team reach the NCAA Final Four in 1998 and 2000.
*Shannon's motto is, "Dream big, believe in yourself, and have fun."

MARY MCVEIGH #22

THE BASICS:

Team: Philadelphia Charge
Position: Midfielder
College: Dartmouth
Hometown: Northampton, MA
Born: November 1, 1981 Philadelphia, PA
Height: 5' 9"

IMPRESSIVE FACTS:

Selected member of 2001 and 2002 All-Ivy First Team...recipient of the 2000 Mickey Price/Keith Kurowsi Award for Contributions on and off the field.
*Mary's favorite TV show is "Dawson's Creek." Her favorite food is a good steak.

MAREN MEINERT #6

THE BASICS:

Team: Boston Breakers
Position: Forward/Midfielder
College: University of Sports (Germany)
Hometown: Duisberg, Germany
Born: August 5, 1973 Duisburg, Germany
Height: 5' 6"

IMPRESSIVE FACTS:

Final thesis for certification in physical education at the University of Sports (Cologne) will be on the history of the WUSA...was a member of the German national team that won the Bronze Medal in the 2000 Olympics in Sydney, Australia...debuted with the German National team at age 15 in Belgium.

TIFFENY MILBRETT #15

THE BASICS:

Team: New York Power
Position: Forward
College: University of Portland
Hometown: Portland, OR
Born: October 23, 1972 Portland, OR
Height: 5' 2"

IMPRESSIVE FACTS:

Majored in communications management and minored in German at the University of Portland...2001 WUSA Most Valuable Player...her high school (Hillsboro High) named their soccer field after her.
*Tiffeny likes to listen to Stevie Nicks and Sarah McLachlan.

HEATHER MITTS #13

THE BASICS:

Team: Philadelphia Charge
Position: Defender
College: University of Florida
Hometown: Cincinnati, OH
Born: June 9, 1978 Cincinnati, OH
Height: 5' 5"

IMPRESSIVE FACTS:

Graduated from Florida in December 2000 with a degree in advertising…has served as a color commentator for SEC soccer games aired on The Sunshine Network.
*Heather's favorite soccer player is Danielle Fotopolous. Her hobbies include golf, tennis, and watching sports on TV.

CARRIE MOORE #5

THE BASICS:

Team: Washington Freedom
Position: Defender
College: William & Mary
Hometown: Roanoke, VA
Born: July 22, 1978 Roanoke, VA
Height: 5' 4"

IMPRESSIVE FACTS:

Majored in kinesiology at the College of William and Mary…started in 16 games for the Freedom in 2002, playing in 18.
*Carrie's favorite book is *A Prayer for Owen Meany* by John Irving. Her motto is, "Try your hardest at everything you do."

MELISSA MOORE #1

THE BASICS:

Team: Philadelphia Charge
Position: Goalkeeper
College: University of New Mexico
Hometown: La Verne, CA
Born: July 17, 1975 Van Nuys, CA
Height: 5' 9"

IMPRESSIVE FACTS:

Graduated from New Mexico in 1997 with a degree in psychology...earned a masters degree in athletic administration from Illinois State University...served as a graduate assistant coach for the women's team while at Illinois State...recorded her longest scoreless streak of the 2002 season at 188 minutes between June 14th and June 24th.

*Melissa's favorite movie is *Life as a House*.

SIRI MULLINIX #18

THE BASICS:

Team: Washington Freedom
Position: Goalkeeper
College: University of North Carolina at Chapel Hill
Hometown: Greensboro, NC
Born: May 22, 1978 Denver, CO
Height: 5' 8"

IMPRESSIVE FACTS:

Majored in exercise and sports science at the University of North Carolina...helped lead the Freedom to the 2002 playoffs with a record 13-save game against Boston on June 1, 2002.

*Siri likes to read any book by Nicholas Sparks. Her nickname is "Dawg."

CARLA OVERBECK #4

THE BASICS:

Team: Carolina Courage
Position: Defender
College: University of North Carolina
at Chapel Hill
Hometown: Chapel Hill, NC
Born: May 9, 1968 Dallas, TX
Height: 5'7"

IMPRESSIVE FACTS:

Won four consecutive NCAA championships as a member of the UNC Tar Heels from 1986-89...did not lose a single game during her tenure at North Carolina...member of the 1991,1995, and 1999 US World Cup teams...mother of two children.

CINDY PARLOW #12

THE BASICS:

Team: Atlanta Beat
Position: Forward
College: University of North Carolina at
Chapel Hill
Hometown: Memphis, TN
Born: May 8, 1978 Memphis, TN
Height: 5'11"

IMPRESSIVE FACTS:

Youngest player to win an Olympic gold medal and a Women's World Cup...awarded the Herman Trophy and the MAC Player of the Year in her senior season at North Carolina.
*Cindy's favorite movie is *The Shawshank Redemption*. Her nickname is "CP."

CHRISTIE PEARCE #3

THE BASICS:

Team: New York Power
Position: Defender
College: Monmouth University
(New Jersey)
Hometown: Point Pleasant, NJ
Born: June 24, 1975 Fort Lauderdale, FL
Height: 5' 6"

IMPRESSIVE FACTS:

Graduated from Monmouth with a degree in special education...had impressive records in both soccer and basketball at Monmouth University in New Jersey.
*Christie has a black Labrador Retriever named Tiger, who can kick a soccer ball.

MARINETTE PICHON #11

THE BASICS:

Team: Philadelphia Charge
Position: Forward
College: Julian Reginier University
(France)
Hometown: Saint Memmie, France
Born: November 26, 1975
Saint Memmie, France
Height: 5' 3"

IMPRESSIVE FACTS:

2002 WUSA Most Valuable Player and Offensive Player of the Year...in 2002 scored the quickest goal in Charge history five minutes into the game against Boston.
*Marinette's pregame ritual is to carry a picture of her family for good luck and to talk to her mother before every game.

BIRGIT PRINZ #9

THE BASICS:

Team: Carolina Courage
Position: Forward
College: Elizabeth Dicka School
(Germany)
Hometown: Frankfurt, Germany
Born: October 25, 1977
Frankfurt, Germany
Height: 5' 9"

IMPRESSIVE FACTS:

Received her degree in massage physiotherapy...electrified the WUSA in 2002, scoring 12 goals and 8 assists in only 15 games...scored the game-winning goal in the 2002 Founders Cup to earn MVP honors...is a member of the German National Team.

HEGE RIISE #10

THE BASICS:

Team: Carolina Courage
Position: Midfielder
Hometown: Lorenskog, Norway
Born: July 18, 1969 Lorenskog, Norway
Height: 5' 6"

IMPRESSIVE FACTS:

Is two-time MVP of the Carolina Courage...one of only three players to earn first team All-WUSA honors in both 2001 and 2002...Captain of Norwegian National Team...won Gold Medal in 1995 FIFA World Cup, 2000 Sydney Olympics, and 1993 UEFA European Championships.

TIFFANY ROBERTS #5

THE BASICS:

Team: Carolina Courage
Position: Defender/Midfielder
College: University of North Carolina
at Chapel Hill
Hometown: San Ramon, CA
Born: May 5, 1977 Petaluma, CA
Height: 5' 3"

IMPRESSIVE FACTS:

Member of the U.S. National Team...guided the Courage to both the regular season and Founders Cup championship as team captain in 2002...has won two World Championships as a member of the 1999 World Cup team and the 1996 Olympic team.
*Tiffany likes to eat sushi and macaroni and cheese.

HOMARE SAWA #8

THE BASICS:

Team: Atlanta Beat
Position: Midfielder
College: Teikyo University (Japan)
Hometown: Tokyo, Japan
Born: September 6, 1978
Tokyo, Japan
Height: 5' 5"

IMPRESSIVE FACTS:

Member of the 2002 All-WUSA first team...January 12, 2003, played the full 90 minutes against the U.S. in a 0-0 game... helped lead Japan to 3rd place in the 14th Asian Games in 2003...member of Japan's 1995 and 1999 Women's World Cup teams.
*Homare has a yellow Labrador named Cobi.

BRIANA SCURRY #1

THE BASICS:

Team: Atlanta Beat
Position: Goalkeeper
College: University of Massachusetts
Hometown: Dayton, MN
Born: September 7, 1971
         Minneapolis, MN
Height: 5'8"

IMPRESSIVE FACTS:

Graduated in 1995 from The University of Massachussetts with a Political Science degree...voted the top female athlete in Minnesota her senior year of high school...made a penalty kick save on China's third shot, helping the U.S. win the 1999 World Cup.
*Briana likes to read any book by James Patterson.

LIFE BEYOND THE WUSA:

Volunteer for the Make A Wish Foundation.

SISSI #10

THE BASICS:

Full Name: Sisleide do Amor Lima
Team: San Jose CyberRays
Position: Midfielder
Hometown: Sao Paulo, Brazil
Born: June 2, 1967 Esplanada, Brazil
Height: 5' 5"

IMPRESSIVE FACTS:

Sissi is a former school teacher...named to the All-WUSA First Team in 2001 and 2002...named 2002 WUSA Humanitarian of the Year...co-scoring leader in the 1999 Women's World Cup with seven goals.
*Sissi likes to "pigout" at McDonald's®.

DANIELLE SLATON #17

THE BASICS:

Team: Carolina Courage
Position: Defender
College: Santa Clara University
Hometown: San Jose, CA
Born: June 10, 1980 San Jose, CA
Height: 5'6"

IMPRESSIVE FACTS:

Youngest member of the U.S. Olympic Team that won a silver medal in the 2000 Summer Olympics in Sydney, Australia...2002 WUSA Defender of the Year.
*Danielle's favorite piece of jewelry is a beaded necklace. Her motto is, "Have no regrets. Live life every day to the fullest and do the best you can for that day."

KATE SOBRERO #15

THE BASICS:

Team: Boston Breakers
Position: Defender
College: Notre Dame
Hometown: Bloomfield Hills, MI
Born: August 23, 1976 Pontiac, MI
Height: 5' 7"

IMPRESSIVE FACTS:

Earned her degree in science/business at Notre Dame...named 2002 Breakers Defender of the Year...starting Defender for the 2000 Olympic team...threw out the first ball at a Detroit Tigers game following the Women's World Cup...worked as an intern at MTV in New York, in 2002.
*Kate's nickname is "SOBS."

HOPE SOLO #18

THE BASICS:

Team: Philadelphia Charge
Position: Goalkeeper
College: University of Washington
Hometown: Richland, WA
Born: July 30, 1981 Richland, WA
Height: 5' 9"

IMPRESSIVE FACTS:

Majored in speech communications...a two-time *Parade Magazine* high school All-American, listed among the nation's finest prep players (1997, 98)...graduated from high school with a 3.70 GPA.
*Hope's favorite TV show is "Will and Grace."

JENNIFER TIETJEN-PROZZO #25

THE BASICS:

Team: Philadelphia Charge
Position: Defender/ Midfielder
College: University of Connecticut
Hometown: Southington, CT
Born: July 14, 1977 Mineola, NY
Height: 5' 9"

IMPRESSIVE FACTS:

Graduated from Connecticut in December 1999 with a degree in kinesiology/exercise science...2003 First-Team All-WUSA player...has been captain on every sports team since high school, including captain of the Charge in 2002, and 2003.
*Jennifer's favorite band is the Dave Matthews Band. She has an identical twin sister, Margaret, who plays for the New York Power.

TISHA VENTURINI-HOCH   #15

THE BASICS:

Team: San Jose CyberRays
Position: Midfielder
College: University of North Carolina
at Chapel Hill
Hometown: Newport Beach, CA
Born: March 3, 1973 Modesto, CA
Height: 5' 6"

IMPRESSIVE FACTS:

Tisha is one of 3 players (including Tiffany Roberts and Carla Overbeck) in women's soccer to win an NCAA title, an Olympic gold medal, the Women's World Cup, and the Founders Cup.

LIFE BEYOND THE WUSA:

Venturini-Hoch is involved with the Children's Crisis Center in Modesto, California.

ALY WAGNER #10

THE BASICS:

Team: San Diego Spirit
Position: Midfielder
College: Santa Clara University
Hometown: San Jose, CA
Born: August 10, 1980 San Jose, CA
Height: 5'5"

IMPRESSIVE FACTS:

Majored in combined sciences...became the first women's high school soccer player to be named Gatorade® Athlete of the Year...first overall pick in 2003 WUSA draft.
*Aly's favorite movies are, *Meet Joe Black* and *Magnolia*.

ABBY WAMBACH #28

THE BASICS:

Team: Washington Freedom
Position: Forward
College: University of Florida
Hometown: Rochester, NY
Born: June 2, 1980 Pittsford, NY
Height: 5'10"

IMPRESSIVE FACTS:

The University of Florida's most prolific scorer ever...Wambach owns school records for goals (96), assists (49), points (241), game-winning goals (24), and hat tricks (10)...was the Freedom's top selection in the 2002 WUSA draft.
*Abby's favorite book is *The Celestine Prophecy*, by James Redfield.

CHRISTIE WELSH #0

THE BASICS:

Team: New York Power
Position: Forward
College: Penn State
Hometown: Massapequa Park, NY
Born: February 27, 1981
Massapequa Park, NY
Height: 5' 10"

IMPRESSIVE FACTS:

Is a Human Development and Family Studies major at Penn State...was drafted in the 1st round, 2nd overall in the 2003 entry draft.
*Christie's favorite book is *Sacred Hoops: Spiritual Lessons of a Hardwood Warrior*, by Phil Jackson. Her favorite movie is *Steel Magnolias*.

CALLIE WITHERS #33

THE BASICS:

Team: Atlanta Beat
Position: Midfielder
College: Stanford University
Hometown: Los Altos Hills, CA
Born: May 29, 1981 Los Altos Hills, CA
Height: 5' 9"

IMPRESSIVE FACTS:

While at Stanford, Callie was a human biology major and art studio minor...was the Atlanta Beat's first pick of the 2003 draft.
*Callie's favorite hobbies are laughing with friends, meditating, painting, drawing, and reading.

The WUSA

Founded by Chairman and CEO of Discovery Communications, John Hendricks, the Women's United Soccer Association was based on the success of a very special group of female soccer athletes who took gold at the 1996 Olympics, won the 1999 FIFA Women's World Cup and earned a silver medal at the 2000 Olympics in Sydney, Australia.

After conducting a comprehensive research analysis and creating a progressive business plan, major American media companies and individual investors joined forces with the nation's leading female soccer stars to form the WUSA on February 15, 2000. Two months later, the league's eight markets were selected and the WUSA finished out the year by signing the majority of the Women's Cup '99 stars to contracts, including every member of the winning American squad.

The WUSA kicked off on April 14, 2001, with the Washington Freedom defeating the Bay Area CyberRays 1-0 in front of 34,148 fans at RFK Stadium. An average of 8,116 fans attended WUSA matches during the league's inaugural season, an astounding 25 percent more than the league's original projections.

The first season was highlighted by the Bay Area CyberRays winning the inaugural WUSA Founders Cup in a penalty kick shootout over the Atlanta Beat following a 3-3 draw during regulation play.

The 2002 WUSA season was capped by the Carolina Courage who rebounded from a dismal 2001 season to claim the 2002 regular season crown and Founders Cup II. More than 15,000 fans witnessed a thrilling match between Carolina and Washington in Founders Cup II on August 24 at Herndon Stadium in Atlanta. Despite a late charge by Hamm and her Washington teammates, Birgit Prinz led the Courage to a 3-2 victory over the Freedom, recording the game-winning goal.

After three exciting seasons, The WUSA has answered the skeptics, becoming unquestionably the world's most elite women's soccer league, with a dynamic and unique collection of female athletes.

More information on the WUSA can be found at www.WUSA.com.

DVD Introduction

The *WUSA Girls Guide to Soccer Life* DVD includes comments from top WUSA players such as Brandi Chastain, Mia Hamm, Julie Foudy, and Tiffeny Milbrett. Watch as they discuss how important the WUSA league is to the fans and to themselves. Hear from National Team Goalkeeper Briana Scurry, founding team member Cindy Parlow, Canadian National Team member Charmaine Hooper, and Atlanta Beat Defender Kylie Bivens, as they chat about getting started in the game, avoiding burnout, overcoming obstacles, and even hair and skin care tips. Listen as they describe their most embarrassing moments. Relive some of the magical moments from the first two seasons of the WUSA league, including highlights of great goals and spectacular saves, as well as standout plays from the Founder's Cup I and II.

DVD MENU

- Play All
- Introduction
- Getting Started
- Game Action
- Valuable Advice
- Great Goals
- Avoiding Burn Out
- Spectacular Saves
- Overcoming Obstacles
- Hard Play
- Hair and Skin Tips
- My Most Embarrassing Moment
- Founder's Cup Highlights